ANGRY LIKE ME

7 Ways to Beat Your Anger Habit… <u>Not</u> Your Neighbor!

Based on the author's own personal battle with Anger, this powerful guide shows you the path to a happier, less frustrating life, free of the physical and verbal aggression that destroys lives.

David Haviland

Copyright © 2018 David Haviland
All rights reserved. This book or any portion thereof may not be reproduced or used in any manner whatsoever without the express written permission of the publisher except for the use of brief quotations in a book review.

Printed in the United States of America
First Printing, 2019
ISBN-13: 9781092124157
ISBN-10: 1092124152
Publisher: David Haviland

Typeset by Amnet Systems.
Cover design by Amnet Systems.

10 9 8 7 6 5 4 3 2 1

DEDICATION

*I dedicate this book to my beloved wife Debbie whose
love, support and amazing artistry have made her the light of my life!
And to my beloved mother Muriel who showed me the path to God.*

CONTENTS

Introduction		vii
Chapter 1	Pissed Off? You & Me Both!	1
Chapter 2	Anatomy Of The Heart Of Anger	5
Chapter 3	Enter The Mindfulness Pyramid	22
Chapter 4	A Glance Into Anger's Broken Mirror	39
Chapter 5	Pulling The Plug On Anger	53
Chapter 6	Turning The Anger Kaleidoscope	77
Chapter 7	Be Assertive, Not Aggressive	96
Chapter 8	Take-Aways From Angry Like Me	107
Overview		117
About the Author		119

INTRODUCTION

So here you are. Plain old tired of being angry all the time. Sick of allowing your inner frustrations, rage, even fury to bubble over into nasty encounters with your mate... hot headed confrontations at work... finger flicking, screaming matches on the road... and even those occasional aggressive altercations that could end up destroying your marriage, alienating your friends and family, costing you your job, or hell – even landing you in jail.

In Angry Like Me, I am right there with you. Every step of the damn way. And I used to suffer terribly because of my own inability to shed the yoke of Anger. It controlled me from the time I woke up, till my head hit the pillow at night. But not anymore.

Did I experience some miraculous cure at a Holy site? Did I get hit by a lightning bolt? Or maybe undergo brain surgery to have my Anger gene removed? Nope. None of the above.

What I did do is step outside myself and decide to make a change. To stop allowing this weakness, affliction, mood disorder – whatever you want to call it – from ruining my life. Causing me to suffer consequences that were painful and costly.

The road is not easy to travel. It takes some real determination and self examination.

But I am here to tell you that if you have the will… I have the way. Ready to take the journey toward a happier, less rageful, less angry life? Let me open the door.

David Haviland, LCSW-R
Licensed Psychotherapist

CHAPTER 1

PISSED OFF? YOU & ME BOTH!

Sure. I know exactly how you feel. It's soooo easy to get angry. To get pissed off. Even red-faced furious in America today. The triggers are everywhere!

You know the drill. You've stopped for a quick bite at your local fast food restaurant. The old guy in front of you can't decide whether he wants a Big Mac or a Fish Sandwich. Or maybe just an egg sandwich. Or maybe just a large fries. And by the way, he asks, shouldn't he be getting a special discount because he's a senior citizen?

At first you just bite your lip and look at your watch. You only get a stinking half hour for lunch at your lousy job and this jerk is using up half of it hemming and hawing and mumbling right in front of you. Now you start shifting from foot to foot, standing there shaking your head, sighing out loud and cursing under your breath... wanting to literally shake this "idiot" in front of you right out of his shoes! Or at least give him a piece of your mind!

Who the hell does he think he is? Standing there at the FAST food counter right in the middle of the lunch time crunch NOT KNOWING WHAT HE WANTS TO ORDER!!!! The nerve of him!

Shouldn't he have known before he got up there on line?? Suddenly your demon mind clicks in and you start visualizing: God, just one quick smack in the head might knock some sense into this slow moving SOB. And who cares if his Big Mac, fries and soft drink careen all over the floor. Dammit to hell! You'll teach him to pull this crap on your time...

And *then* — just as suddenly as your fury hits a fever pitch — you hear the cashier say the words "Next customer please." And the storm has suddenly passed. You relax. Your blood pressure subsides. You order your lunch. The visions of fury and homicidal rage are gone. You're OK now. You eat, head back to work, you're chill. Until, that is, the next "idiot' crosses your path.

And the cycle starts up all over again... because these people are everywhere! On the road driving in front of you. Sitting in the seat in front of you at the movie theater. Talking too loud at the library. Speaking on their cell phones on the morning train. Fishing for coupons on the checkout line at the supermarket. It's like these knuckleheads were put on this planet just to torture people like you and me.

As an Anger Addict myself, I fully understand that fantasy image of knocking that slow poke's Big Mac on the floor and watching him clean it up! Or driving my pick up right into that little subcompact who just cut me off, and pushing him off the damn highway. That SOB won't cut me off again! Or taking a baseball bat to that music freak's stereo up on the 3rd floor. Let's see how he likes the sound of cracking plastic at 1 o'clock in the morning!

Justice must be served. My rage must be unleashed. Fashioning myself as the self righteous punisher, I could level swift judgments against virtually anyone who crossed my path. There was never a day when I didn't find someone who was too slow... too thoughtless... too stupid... too inconsiderate. And I was always right, and they were always wrong.

God, the addiction to my Anger and the thrill of always being right felt so good at a gut level. It was a heady experience... like a special high. I was always vigilant for opportunities to attack. Or at least unleash some of my self righteous fury! Nothing felt better, that's for sure.

UNTIL ONE DAY I REALIZED THAT MY ANGER SAID <u>WAAAAY MORE ABOUT ME</u> THAN ABOUT THE PEOPLE AROUND ME!!!

How, you ask, can a Licensed Psychotherapist, respected by his patients and colleagues alike, with years of experience in the Mental Health field have an Anger problem? Same way your everyday Pastor, Police Officer, Electrician, School Teacher, Judge, Plumber, Doctor, Librarian, Nurse, Astronaut, Deep Sea Diver, Attorney, Truck Driver and Zoologist can – The Anger Addiction knows no particular race, creed, color, career choice or social status. We may be completely different people. And the roots of our Anger might differ. But the urge to fuel the addiction is the same. It simply feels good when we allow the Anger to vent itself because it's a pressure that always demands release.

The real problem is that the more we engage in blindly RELEASING our Anger... through either nasty, caustic responses, vicious verbal attacks or physical violence, the more we blind ourselves to the roots of the fury inside us. And the more likely we are to suffer the consequences of our Anger.

Yes! At a very basic level, you and I <u>do</u> understand that it isn't as much about that "idiot" in line as it is about our own relentless urge to be pissed off, to criticize, to correct, to humiliate, to throttle, to punch, to punish, to dump our own rage and fury which seem to bubble always to the surface.

And those consequences I mentioned? They can range from destroying relationships with loved ones and pissing off coworkers... to losing jobs, getting thrown out of school, busting up friendships, getting fined, arrested, and even going to jail or prison – for years!!!

While feeling Anger, or at least frustration with things around us, is a normal part of being a person in today's world, it certainly doesn't have to be a constant, controlling companion in our lives. And it certainly doesn't have to lead to physical or verbal aggression. If you're reading this book, I figure you want to A. Find ways to control your own personal Anger and reduce its influence on your life, B. Learn why you are so angry in the first place and, C. Avoid the "Big C" which is the Consequences of Anger.

Until you and I get to that point, here's to feeling the temporary rush and exhilaration of exploding on someone in line... chasing down someone who cuts you off on the highway... making your spouse cry and feel two inches tall... or popping somebody in the face when they get in the way of your plans.

But if you're ready to accept the challenge of changing your world – and enjoying all the benefits of an Anger-Free life – let's beat this Anger Addiction together!

CHAPTER 2

ANATOMY OF THE HEART OF ANGER

What exactly is Anger? What does it look like? What does it smell like? Where does it come from? If you're like me, Anger is such a hard-wired, instant, spontaneous impulse that you are rarely even aware of how it sneaks up on you. You get this fuzzy, unsettled feeling. Your mind goes numb. Alarms and bells and warning lights start blasting in your head. And "Wham" you're angry! Your demon mind then goes into hyper drive, searching for the meanest, most vindictive, evil, paralyzing thing you can do to the person or thing that has upset you.

But here's the good news. Just *feeling* angry doesn't mean that you automatically have to launch into nuclear attack mode. Or any form of attack for that matter, physical or verbal. By recognizing what it is that really gets your blood boiling, knowing the exact trigger that gets you to see red, you can corral that raging, powerful impulse and squelch its urge for expression. You can even begin to look at the source of your anger differently, with less frustration. And in many cases, you can actually avoid putting yourself in the kinds of situations that might lead you to a verbal or physical expression of your Anger in the first place. We'll be looking for ways to help you achieve that as you move forward in this book.

Without a conscious, pre-calculated awareness of what triggers you… there is a high likelihood that you will explode in a barrage of middle-finger-pointing, F word cursing, fist clenching, kick ass shouting rage. Or maybe even let your target feel your physical wrath with a punch in the face or a kick to the gut. Or maybe take a baseball bat and knock the headlights out on his car. And you and your victim are left to pick up the pieces. The best way to get ahold of this mysterious and volatile emotion is to freeze frame it with a snapshot that says "Ah, so that's what I look like when my Anger begins to surge inside me and screams to be released." That moment when someone cuts you off. Or makes you wait in line. Or appears to be disrespectful. And that fuzzy feeling starts creeping up on you. It may sound hokey but doing so enables you to study the details. Examine your reaction from every angle. Once you are mindful in this way of Anger's presence, you can identify your specific triggers and those situations that are most likely to ignite it, while committing yourself to watching the Anger unfold, scene by scene, from that tiny wiff of resentment to the urge for the red-faced explosion that often follows.

Doing this is often far more challenging than one might imagine. Think of it almost like breathing. You are breathing all day long, sometimes faster, sometimes slower but you're never really conscious of it going on – at least not unless you focus on it. Breathing is a function that is pretty much on automatic pilot.

For many of us, Anger is a lot like that. On automatic pilot. When we're not mentally aware of its presence and vigilant about controlling it, Anger is kind of an invisible aura around us. Simmering. Invisible. Like a cloud of poison flammable gas, the presence of Anger often hangs over us unseen and unnoticed. And the expression of Anger is often detonated so instantly and unconsciously during the course of our day, that it strikes like a rocket… and we are left standing there, observing the carnage like a witness to a brutal car accident. We experienced that angry pressure, unleashed the anger, felt the release but it almost seemed like we were controlled by the Anger rather than the other way around.

Think about it. When we laugh or tell a joke, we are in control. We're also in control when we talk about our favorite sports team. When we decide to have steak rather than chicken for dinner, we are in control. Same thing when we choose to watch a scary movie and be frightened. Or decide to call a friend and share happy moments. At those times we are pretty much always in control.

But in this current world where your Anger controls you, it's almost like you're constantly treading through a dangerous minefield, not seeing the lethal explosives that lie beneath the surface. Every waking hour, all around you may seem fine, but you never know whether you will get through the day unscathed, or blow your freaking leg off! By recognizing the events and experiences that are most likely to trigger you to that feeling of anger, you become more actively aware of those "explosive" situations, people and events... and are way *more* likely to be able to pull the plug before you act with physical or verbal aggression.

Talk about recognizing our own personal minefields, all of this discussion reminds me of a story I heard about an event that occurred down south a few years back. The event concerned a man who actually had his own *farm* fields, and every spring he would plant acres of beautiful sunflowers which he would sell to shopkeepers in the neighboring villages. As he often did over the years, this man was said to have tractored the land, planted the seeds, and then, after several days of hard work, he'd string up some loose wire fence and tape paper signs every few yards telling passers by to "Keep Off." It was important to do this, so the seed had a chance to take root and grow into the gorgeous sunflowers which would fetch him a pretty penny and augment his income during the summer months.

Now it happened that a group of horse enthusiasts in the area apparently took a shine to that particular ridge of land. And one night, under a dazzling full moon, three of them decided to jump over the loose wire fence, and race their stallions across the freshly planted land, tearing it to pieces in the process. When the owner arrived the next day, and witnessed the damage to his land, he was really, really pissed off. After all his hard work, and several thousand dollars of his money, these horseback riders had ignored his signs, crashed through his fence, and wreaked havoc on his land. The damage was so bad that the land would have to be seeded all over again.

Now, remember what I said about that "hard-wired, spontaneous impulse" and that "fuzzy, unsettled" feeling? Imagine how YOU yourself would have felt under these crappy circumstances. If you weren't pissed off there'd likely be something wrong with you. Of course the owner was pissed off. That's a given. It cost him a ton of time, hard work and money. But it's what he did *next* that created a world of pain for him, even though he was clearly the victim in this awful situation.

Feeling the Anger and acting on it are two very different things. This man had struggled with Anger related to his farming work in the past. His farm was the most important thing in his life and naturally he had difficulty tolerating any disrespect or actual abuse toward it. Perhaps his intolerance was based on the fact that he'd watched his father, also a farmer, lose his land to the banks when his crops failed and he had no money to pay his mortgage. That simple painful experience may have been enough to plant the seed of Anger inside him, and made him just a little more likely to feel frustration and even rage when it came to any issues relating to his own land. And he truly did feel this Anger... and in the past there were many events that might have moved him from *feeling* the Anger to *acting* on it.

There was that time a neighboring farmer had failed to keep his cattle from wandering over onto this man's land, and they grazed there for several days eating grass that was meant for his own cows. There was also the time that the power company drove trucks on his land to fix some powerlines right after he had seeded several years before. In both of these particular cases, he was very angry, and totally pissed off. Rightfully so. He may have daydreamed of dealing with these problems by showing up with his shotgun in hand. Or setting his neighbor's farmhouse on fire. Or slashing the tires of the Power Company trucks when the workmen went home for the night. But he took action in ways that did not unleash physical or verbal aggression. By recognizing that "fuzzy, unsettled" feeling of Anger – and then choosing <u>NOT</u> to let those feelings carry him toward physical or verbal violence – he was able to resolve both issues using an assertive response, calling on the phone and complaining sternly but calmly in each case. The result: His neighbor paid him for the grass that his cattle ate… and the Power Company reimbursed him for the damage they had done. No further hassle, and absolutely <u>no consequences</u> – something that surely would have happened had he chosen to physically or verbally express his displeasure! Had he allowed his Anger to control <u>him</u>… rather than the other way around.

Oh boy! Sadly enough, in the case of the horseback riders, he failed to remember how the assertive approach had served him so well in the past with his other farm-related issues. Feeling disrespected, downtrodden and totally dissed, this time he gave into that "fuzzy, unsettled" feeling that propelled him toward rage. He acted in a way that reflected the extreme Anger he felt inside. Had he stopped for an instant and freeze-framed that moment with a snapshot of his angry moment as I talked about earlier, he would have A. realized that this wasn't the first time he'd been involved in Anger provoking situations related to his farming life and B. he would have remembered that people showing disrespect for his land was a primary trigger to Anger (perhaps planted in his heart and mind years ago by the suffering of his father)… but one that had been dealt with effectively in the past. Likely he would have then grabbed hold of himself, and simply called the neighbors with the horses and asked for compensation. Or even photographed the ravaged land and then called the police and his attorney, allowing them to settle the problem.

But that's not what happened. Giving vent to the growing rage inside him, the land owner went down to the neighbor's home, listening to his demon mind, and drove his big four wheel drive truck right up to their corral about an hour after midnight. He opened the gates and then let his Anger get the better of him. I believe he fired his shotgun three times in the air...scattering the horses... and fired once or twice at the house, terrifying the neighbors out of a deep sleep. Within seconds the local police pulled into the driveway behind him. Oops! He paid a high price for the release of his righteous Anger: a month in county jail and compensation for chasing his neighbors' horses and disturbing the peace. Wow! Talk about consequences. Consequences! Consequences! All because he was unable to avoid running into that minefield. His own personal minefield of feeling angry at being disrespected... especially as it relates to his work on the farm.

That's his story. How well do you recognize your own minefield? And how capable are you of "freeze framing" your feelings and pulling the plug on your Anger before you unleash a raging inferno of aggression? Does something your spouse does – like leaving dishes in the sink or writing checks without telling you – leave your Anger screaming for expression in the form of hurtful, humiliating words leaving your marriage on the brink of destruction? Does a coworker's carelessness or lateness drive you up the wall, leaving your Anger screaming to be released in the form of a vicious tirade in front of fellow colleagues? Does your resentment at a neighbor's barking dog push you to the edge, causing you to "bubble over" with plans to get even with that SOB? Try the following little scenario on for size and see if it doesn't reflect how quickly and almost unexpectedly the feeling and expression of Anger could change <u>your</u> life.

So you've had a great day at work. Your boss gives you a compliment. In fact, he's so impressed with your performance that he's giving you a substantial raise. You can't wait to call your spouse and share the good news. You call your favorite restaurant and make reservations for dinner to celebrate. You even stop to get flowers. You're about to pull into your driveway to share all that happiness with your spouse when BAM! You see a scratch in the side of your spouse's new car. The one you just made a hefty monthly payment on.

You jump out of your car. Run up to survey the damage. "Dammit to hell!!" you scream, without even asking what happened. "Was anyone hurt? How did it occur? Are your loved ones safe and OK?" No, you don't ask those questions. You are locked and loaded, ragefully upset about how this affects YOU. Suddenly your Anger is controlling you. Your spouse is a crappy driver. How dare she do this to you? An argument with your spouse ensues. You humiliate her in front of everyone. The kids start crying. Your whole night and the celebration you had planned are now ruined. Your Anger has controlled you once again.

Sound familiar? It surely does if you are in the "Anger Controls Me" mode. That's why the first step to a better life is taking that "snapshot" and watching our Anger happen to us in real time. It reveals what our triggers are, how quickly we lose control, how pissed off we get – from just a little all the way up to a nuclear blast. Watching, or monitoring our Anger with a snapshot in real time lets us gather information that will later help us to stand back and say "Wow! Look at me. Yes, I am unhappy about the scratch in the new car. My heart is pumping and I'm feeling flushed as my Anger surges. Underneath it all, it probably stirs up those old, deep-seated feelings of rage I felt toward my older brother Tom who'd steal the shiny bike I got for Christmas and ride it carelessly, breaking spokes and flattening the tires. But that was then. This is now. Let me think about this situation for a second. I love my spouse who does so much for me and our family. Losing her in the accident would have been the REAL tragedy. But she's OK. Accidents happen. She didn't intentionally do this to ruin my day. As painful as it feels for me at this moment, I do have insurance to handle accidents like this. I will not allow my immediate feelings to control me, destroying and derailing all the other plans, feelings and objectives that had been in my mind prior to the upsetting event or experience." It's like watching a crash scene. Together let's find out how we can put on the brakes and avoid that "crash" from happening again and again.

Mindfulness starts with determining what experiences ignite our particular brand of Anger in the first place. And holding the image of that frustration and potential explosion, real or imagined in your mind's eye. My most lethal trigger – the match that lights my fuse and could very easily lead to an explosion – has all to do with my perception of people wasting my time, testing my patience, basically being inconsiderate of me from a time perspective.

Underneath it all, it can probably be traced to the fact that growing up, I was one of eleven kids in a family where my parents barely kept their heads above water financially. The only thing that was bountiful in our house other than love was scarcity. Can you imagine what it's like waiting for a small meatloaf to make its way around the dinner table when 10 other people have access to the platter first??!! Not a real patience builder. And sharing the bathroom when several other siblings are waiting urgently in line ahead of you. Not good for building patience either. It's not rocket science. The frustrations and painful experiences of childhood often have a direct correlation to the frustration, and short-fused Anger that we exhibit as adults.

For some of us, it's rooted in that powerless feeling and lack of control we may have experienced when an older sibling or a parent disrespected us or took away something important to us. Like stealing and damaging our shiny new bike or grounding us every day for a month because they suspected us of something we didn't do. Sometimes it's the negative demeanor of a rageful parent who becomes our role model. Cursing and swearing at everything from a dirty coffee cup and the garbage not being taken out, to making out the check to "the damned cable company." When we grow up, we act similarly, figuring well, that's just the way adults act. Other times it's the verbal, physical or even sexual abuse we suffer as children that gives us that angry edge where we see the world as a threatening and hostile place. "Nobody will ever hurt or put one over on me again," we say. And we remain in vigilant attack mode. Our seething hostility is our red badge of self righteousness. The trigger is always cocked, just surveying the landscape for the next potential target of our wrath. And then there's the frustration of being demeaned as a child, being made to wait, being made to feel "unimportant" or "stupid" which shows itself in adulthood when we project our inner rage – the rage we couldn't direct toward the powerful adults who hurt us — onto those intolerable traffic jams, standing in line at the grocery store, or situations where we feel slighted, humiliated or made to feel "less than" by bosses, colleagues, spouses or others. Looking back at why we struggle with anger can lead to understanding and greater control. And we all have different journeys.

In my particular case, I need to be mindful of my lack of patience and anticipate that certain places (like doctors' offices, supermarket lines, and bank lines during rush hour) must be handled with ultra special care. So if I walk into my local Shoprite store at 11:30 on a Saturday morning when I know I have a 12 noon patient appointment 8 miles away, I'm just asking for trouble. I've taken those visual "snapshots" of myself and seen what waiting in line, or being delayed in some other way does to my mind and my body. I start looking and feeling frustrated, hyperactive, disrespected. I shift from foot to foot. I look heavenward as if hoping to be delivered from the "idiots" around me. Sighing and groaning is my MO as I stand behind someone in line I deem to be "too slow." (Remember me watching the meatloaf moving so slowly around the table as a child? Worrying that I might not get any?) My mindfulness of my Anger vulnerability in that situation dictates that I need to calm down, recognize that this is a major trigger for me, resolve not to allow my anger to bubble forth in aggression, and ultimately to avoid that experience in the future like the plague. And believe me, I have learned to do so! Going to the supermarket after 9 o'clock at night usually eliminates the possibility I'll flip out and be physically or verbally aggressive.

If you're like the person in our little "job-celebration-turned-sour-by-car-accident" story earlier, you may not give a damn about being delayed in a grocery line, or waiting an hour in a Doctor's office lobby. But God help the person who dares to cost you money through stupidity, misfortune, lack of concern, or a cavalier indifference to the fact that you kill yourself for a living and simply CAN'T handle things like car scrapes and dents going wrong in your life!

You know who you are. But probably you don't know how close you always are to an Angry explosion simply because being mindful of your worst triggers has never been something you've practiced. You've never made it a priority til now.

Test Your Anger Control IQ
Are You smart and savvy enough to control your Anger? Or does that red faced, red eyed, steaming, snarling Anger Monster control you? Take this revealing Quiz and find out just how much control you have… or don't have.

Scenario 1:
OK so you own a flower farm. You've just spent a thousand bucks to plow 10 acres of your land and plant sunflowers and tulips and daisies which will blossom soon. You even put a wire fence around the land with signs saying "Keep Off." The next day you see that the fence is down, and the folks from the house down the hill have raced their thoroughbred horses all over your land.

You are clearly upset. First thing you do is:

1. Take an aspirin, lie down and do the breathing exercises & meditations in Chapter 5
2. Take photos of the damage, call the local police, & then get in touch with your attorney
3. Pick up the phone and start threatening to beat the daylights out of your neighbors
4. Head down to the neighbor's house and fire a shotgun scattering their horses

Your answer: _____

Scenario 2:
So you found a quiet seat on the morning train and you settle in to enjoy your coffee and the morning newspaper. Suddenly a person in a loud tee shirt wearing headphones slides into the seat right next to you, blasting the latest rock music at a level that is both audible and annoying. As hard as you try, you are unable to distract yourself from the music and you still have an hour left on the train before your reach your destination.

You are clearly upset. First thing you do is:

1. Get up and move to another train car where you hope to find a quiet seat
2. Ask the person to turn the music down using the assertiveness skills from Chapter 7
3. Turn toward them and threaten to have the conductor throw them off the train
4. Yank the wires from their headphones and toss them on the floor

Your answer: _____

Scenario 3:
You've always had a pretty decent relationship with your elderly next door neighbor. Until one day after his wife passes away, he comes home with a yappy, snappy little dog who does nothing but bark from early morning to late at night. Now you're being awakened by this mutt two hours early every day, and you can't even sit out on your deck without provoking a vicious barking tirade. This dog has turned your once happy home into a house of horrors.

You are clearly upset. First thing you do is:

1. Put your house up for sale and move to another town
2. Write a kind, but firm note to him using the Cognitive Restructuring skills from Chapter 6
3. Call and read him the "riot act" threatening to quiet the little dog "permanently."
4. Wait till your neighbor goes shopping, and then bring the dog to the local pound

Your answer: _____

Scenario 4:
You're at your favorite vacation spot up north, and it's another one of those lazy, hazy days of summer that you and your family used to enjoy. But that was before the Mr. Softee man started parking his truck right across the street from your cabin. Suddenly half the vacation community is congregating within ten feet of your deck. And you and your family now spend evenings picking up the wrappers and popcicle sticks that everyone leaves behind.

You are clearly upset. First thing you do is:

1. Start taking "stay-cations" at home where you know you won't be hassled.
2. After buying some ice cream, kindly suggest an alternate location for his business
3. Tell him he's ruining your vacation, and threaten to call the cops if he doesn't leave
4. Ram your family vehicle into his truck, and push it down the road to a "better" location

Your answer: _____

Scenario 5:
You have just responded to an ad for some part time work at a local supermarket. The supervisor asks you to put on an apron and start stacking cans of soup in aisle 12. You work for about an hour when the supervisor comes up and tells you that he overestimated his need for help this week. He doesn't need you after all and says that he's sorry but he only pays workers who have put in at least six hours on a given day. He suggests you call him again next week.

You are clearly upset. First thing you do is:

1. Text message your friend that you can't believe your bad luck
2. Using skills from Chapter 7, you point out that you put in a full hour and deserve to be paid.
3. Drop the carton of soup cans, and storm out, cursing the manager in a loud voice.
4. Return later that night with friends and TP (toilet paper) the entire building.

Your answer: _____

Scenario 6:
It's a Saturday evening in June. You've had a great day and now you're enjoying a delightful dinner at your local Chinese Restaurant. You and your spouse order the chicken chow mein while the kids go for the sweet and sour pork. Suddenly after a few savory bites from your dish, your jaw drops open. You can't believe your eyes! Your chopsticks reveal a long black hair lying among the bean sprouts.

You are clearly upset. First thing you do is:

1. Push your plate away and say "That's it for me."
2. Quietly summon the waiter and ask for a refund.
3. Express your disgust and loudly threaten to call the Health Department.
4. Storm back to the Manager's office and dump the food on his desk.

Your answer: _____

Scenario 7:
So you've been waiting for weeks for the new Action Heroes movie to debut at your local theater. Now it's finally here. You get tickets for yourself and your spouse and sit down to enjoy the movie. It has all your favorite actors for gosh sake! But suddenly a very tall man wearing an oversized hat sits directly in front of you blocking your view.

You are clearly upset. First thing you do is:

1. Sigh loudly and hope he hears you.
2. Tap him lightly on his shoulder and ask him respectfully to remove his hat.

3. Start complaining loudly about "stupid, insensitive people."
4. Ask him to remove the hat. Then fling it wildly toward the screen when he refuses.

Your answer: _____

Scenario 8:
Your Mom complains that you never do anything around the house. Then one day you surprise her by washing all the dishes and putting them away. Expecting a compliment and a word of thanks, you're shocked when she says "Can't you do anything right?? You put all the coffee cups on the wrong shelf! I would have been better off doing the whole job myself!"

You are clearly upset. First thing you do is:

1. Apologize profusely for being such a dim-witted dunce.
2. Cut your poor, tired Mom some slack using the cognitive restructuring skills in Chapter 6.
3. Tell your Mom to freaking do them herself next time.
4. Grab a coffee cup and hurl it at her in a fit of rage.

Your answer: _____

Scenario 9:
So you've been waiting on line for over 45 minutes at the Department of Motor Vehicles office to turn in old license plates and get your refund. Finally your number – Number 29 – comes up on the screen above you. Your long wait appears to be over. But hold everything! Over the loudspeaker, someone announces: "The DMV will be closed for lunch and will reopen again in thirty minutes. Please hold on to your numbers."

You are clearly upset. First thing you do is:

1. Shrug your shoulders and say "It's the story of my life."
2. Speak to the manager and ask for a break since you have to return to work.
3. Start cursing out the clerical staff as a bunch of "overpaid baboons."
4. Chuck your plates over the window, telling them to "shove em where the sun don't shine."

Your answer: _____

Scenario 10:
It's another morning commute and you're making good time on the two way road you always take to work. Suddenly you reach a point where the car in front of you is crawling at a snail's pace. That's despite the road signs indicating that it is a 45 mile per hour zone. You notice that there's an elderly gentleman behind the wheel. You have plenty of time, but following the elderly man in front of you has you constantly hitting the brakes to avoid a collision.

You are clearly upset. First thing you do is:

1. Sigh and tell yourself that the day was "just too good to be true."
2. Realize that old people have limitations, and use your skills from Chapter 6 to cut frustration.
3. Honk every ten seconds and hope the man is terrified into pulling over.
4. Pass him at lightning speed, almost hitting him, while turning and giving him "the finger."

Your answer: _____

Now tally up your score!!!

If your total is between 25 and 40 points, you have likely come to the right place! You are dwelling in a place where your Anger Monster pretty much controls your life. You see life as a "me vs. them" struggle, and you get pissed off or enraged at many of the challenges you face in everyday life. Unless you scored fewer than 25 points (where you may be passive, self blaming or positively assertive) you are definitely angry like me. And that means you are going through life on the verge of suffering consequences like lost jobs, broken relationships, jail time and worse in virtually every challenging instance you face. It's time to get control of your Anger… and <u>not</u> let it control you. Let's get started!

CHAPTER 3

ENTER THE MINDFULNESS PYRAMID... AND BECOME MINDFULLY AWARE!

It's quite normal to get upset over specific little things during the course of the day. After all you're a human being, not a robot. For example, you just spent $20 to have your car washed and waxed yesterday... and today it's raining. Damn. Or you wear your favorite shoes to work and somehow your right foot steps in a huge wad of bubble gum. Yech. You might be ticked off, peeved or pissed off somewhere along the lower tiers of what I call the Mindfulness Pyramid. Other than a stray curse word, an aggravated sigh, or a head shaking feeling of consternation though, it is probably safe to say that you will likely not rip somebody's head off or go ballistic over those lower tier frustrations. (As the four-level pyramid diagram shows, "Ticked Off" is the least powerful or lowest level of Anger with 1, 2, and 3 shown. It is followed by "Peeved" with the numbers 4, 5, and 6 shown, and then "Pissed Off" with 7,8 and 9 shown as you move up toward the top, peak level of Anger which we'll call "Enraged" with the number 10 shown.)

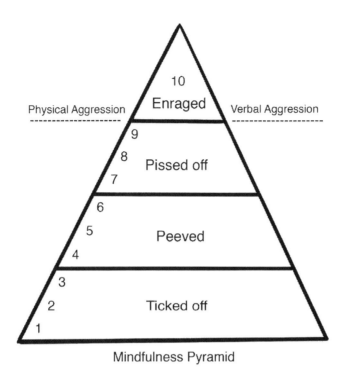

Copyright © 2018 David Haviland

It's that top tier in which the potential for truly explosive Anger resides. It's that moment of physical or verbal aggression and the resulting consequences, that is your Achilles heel, and what you most want to avoid. It's that moment when someone cuts you off on your way to work, and you follow them 8 miles to force a physical confrontation. Or that moment when someone allows their dog to take a crap on your front lawn and you confront him with a baseball bat. Or a neighbor starts cutting their grass at 7 am on a Sunday morning when you're trying to sleep and you respond by driving your truck across his front lawn.

These are just a few of those top tier possibilities in the Mindfulness Pyramid. The real rage triggers – as far as YOU personally are concerned – can range from perceived disrespect and betrayal to outright obnoxious behavior. But YOU must identify, study, examine and acknowledge your very own rage triggers in order to gain the mindfulness that can set you free.

Trust me. You will rapidly become a pro at identifying YOUR OWN Anger triggers. And once you place this Mindfulness Pyramid in your mind, you will give yourself a permanent STOP SIGN that will help you identify those particular events and situations that trigger you to GO HEAD OVER HEELS OVER THE CLIFF before you do!!! You'll also enjoy a clear comparison between those events and situations that simply tick you off... or leave you peeved or pissed off...and those specific situations that could cause you to totally lose it and end up suffering the kind of terrible consequences that we talked about earlier.

In facilitating my own Anger Management Program, and while later working at a mental health clinic, I have used something called an "Anger Meter" which was part of a Federal Government issued booklet in general use entitled Anger Management for Substance Abuse and Mental Health Clients. This "meter" helped provide a very simple way of monitoring one's level of anger. From 1 through 9 (with 1 being the lowest level of anger) you were OK. It was only when you crossed the line into the 10 range that you were likely to experience consequences because at 10 you would have committed either physical or verbal aggression toward another human being. To me this meter left something to be desired because it didn't name the levels of human frustration and anger in a way that people could sink their teeth into. By creating the Mindfulness Pyramid, with specific locations like "Ticked Off" and "Peeved" and "Pissed Off" and "Enraged" I provided a way to measure <u>and</u> compartmentalize specific triggers to help each of us personally create a hierarchy of triggers. Those triggers that found a home at the apex of the Pyramid (The "Enraged" zone) were flagged as being "potentially lethal and toxic" in terms of the repercussions they might bring. Triggers relegated to the lower tiers, were less concerning and actually gave us hope and encouragement that all of our triggers might someday have that little power over us.

I encourage you to use the Mindfulness Pyramid to file your own triggers and Anger "hot spots." But before you do, check out my own personal Mindfulness Pyramid and the things that just tick me off... those that peeve me... those that piss me off and push me to the brink of aggression... and finally those things that can send me careening over the top toward total uncontrollable rage, aggression and the consequences that go with it.

What "Ticks me off?" Little things like just missing a green light. Darn. That might be a 1 on the scale. Or having my gas grill suddenly die in the middle of cooking a hamburger. Ugh. That might be a 2. Or having my local coffee shop run out of my favorite donut. Sheesh.

In my Anger Management groups, I often talk about this one particular situation that ticks me off every time I think about it. So imagine this. I'm out in my yard on a beautiful spring day. The birds are singing. I'm whistling a happy tune, and I'm enjoying the warmth of the sunshine on my face. Everything seems perfect as I rake up the stray leaves that winter left behind. I'm enjoying every aspect of this gorgeous experience until BAM!! I reach into a thicket of branches and my rake displaces a bee hive! Zip, zip, zip! I'm stung once, twice, three times and I run like hell for the shelter of my house. There, amidst a few of my choicest expletives, my lovely, caring wife applies ice cubes to my burning sting bites. Geesh! I needed to hit that bee hive like I needed a hole in my head. My Mindfulness snapshot of myself shows me unhappy, frustrated, in pain, but nowhere near rageful. I accept that bees have a right to live too. I was in the wrong place at the wrong time. But I'm still "Ticked Off."

And here's something else: I didn't go berserk. I didn't inexplicably turn a flame thrower on the poor bees who innocently protected their hive. I didn't suddenly drive to my local supermarket and start bashing the shelves of bottled honey in reprisal. And I didn't race to the nearest beekeeper and burn down all of his hives. Simply put, I just didn't hit that "Enraged" level at the top of the Mindfulness Pyramid.

"Ticked Off" is at the bottom sphere of the Mindfulness Pyramid. Ah, if my Anger could only reside forever in that lowest realm of frustration and consternation. Sure, my reaction to missing that green light might be in the lower sphere of that "Ticked Off" realm (maybe a 1)… compared to a more emotional "Ticked Off" for my reaction to the bee stings (perhaps a 3). But I'm still within the realm of safe, consequence free Anger. It's really OK to be angry in the "Ticked Off" zone. No sweat!

Next let's explore the "Peeved" zone and the events and behaviors that fall into that category for me, yours truly.

To my mind, "Peeved" is a slight step upward from "Ticked Off." "Peeved" which falls in the next sphere up on our Mindfulness Pyramid scale, implies a slightly more intense, slightly hotter reaction to the situation or event itself. Perhaps there is even more thought and judgment involved in being "Peeved." And while it is nowhere near the rage and consequences at the top of the pyramid, it is a realm where perceptions, emotions and responses are occurring with what I'd describe as "extra sizzle!"

Keep in mind that what leaves me "Peeved" may not even touch a nerve with you. You will have plenty of opportunities to see where you fit on the "Peeved" scale. One of my most memorable "Peeved" experiences started, of all places, with a roast beef sandwich! I love roast beef sandwiches and enjoying one when I'm particularly hungry is up there with my favorite culinary experiences of all time.

On this particular occasion I decided to purchase a roast beef hero from the local delicatessen on my way to work. Made to order, this sandwich was a true culinary masterpiece, featuring the most mouthwatering medium rare roast beef, laid on a bed of crisp lettuce and fresh tomatoes and smothered in mayonnaise with a dash of salt and pepper. The crisp Italian bread alone made my mouth water. Mmmm!

When I got to work that particular morning, I placed my neatly wrapped roast beef sandwich in the refrigerator I shared with my fellow colleagues at the clinic. I bid it "goodbye" and through every group therapy session I ran that morning, I dreamt of how wonderful it would be to bite into that luscious roast beef sandwich. To savor every delightful, mouthwatering morsel.

As 12 noon approached, my anticipation reached a fever pitch. As my last group therapy patient headed for the door, I closed my briefcase and headed for the refrigerator to devour that roast beef sandwich!

And that's when it happened! As I opened the door to the refrigerator I shared with my colleagues, the worst possible sight greeted my disbelieving eyes: My beautiful roast beef sandwich was gone, and all that remained were the white deli wrapping papers that had held my prized lunch!

I was "Peeved." Imagine! Someone had the freaking nerve to take my precious sandwich without asking me. I would have gladly shared it had anyone asked. With a stern grimace on my "peeved" face, I raced into the office we shared, demanding to know in the loudest voice possible who had dared to do this to me. Turned out, the sandwich was taken by a visitor to the clinic who somehow thought that the food in the office fridge was available to all. Dumb!

In any case, I didn't grab anyone by the collar. I didn't threaten to stuff the wrapping papers down anyone's throat. I didn't flip anyone's desk over or knock anyone's plants on the floor. There were no threats or physical aggression that would bring about likely consequences.

Being "Peeved" is where losing my roast beef sandwich put me on the Mindfulness Pyramid. Again, as with the "Ticked Off" range of angry moments, the realm of being "Peeved" was safe, relatively hot anger but still under control for me. No aggression. No consequences. Probably a 5 on the scale. "Peeved" is a place of consequence free anger. It's not pleasant, it definitely raises the blood pressure, but it's OK to be angry in the "Peeved" zone.

Another time I fell into the "Peeved" zone started out innocently enough. I had just purchased a beautiful used car on a Friday evening and couldn't wait to impress my buddies at work the following Monday with my shiny, sporty new baby! Problem was that in the short time I had owned it, the car was covered in dust and dirt from a recent thunderstorm, and my baby had lost the magnificent lustre it had when I drove it out of the dealership. When I woke up Sunday morning I made an executive decision. Rather than heading out to the beach or on a picnic with my family on that beautiful, but warm, July Sunday, I decided to scrub, wash, vacuum and wax my beautiful new car. Wait till my buddies see my gorgeous set of wheels tomorrow, I thought, bursting with pride. So under the sunny, 92 degree skies, I worked my fingers to the bone. From 12 noon to nearly sunset, I washed, and dried, and waxed until my baby glistened and glowed in the July sun. Wow, I could see my reflection in my car's beautiful sky blue finish! I had spent almost six and a half hours working in my driveway with hoses and buckets, rags, sprays and wax. But it was well worth it. Wait til my buddies at work set their eyes on my masterpiece!

Next day, I couldn't wait to get behind the wheel of my beauty and drive to work. As I pulled into the parking lot, the radio blared out the weather forecast. "Another scorcher," the announcer said. "95 degrees and sunny today, so stay cool." I looked for the shadiest spot I could find in the parking lot. Pulling into a spot under a large elm tree, I got out and looked back admiringly as I walked toward the office. "Wait til my buddies see you at 5 o'clock," I thought.

The day went well inside our air conditioned office. I reminded two of my buddies to wait for me at 5 so we could walk out together. I had quite a surprise for them.

Well the surprise ended up being on me. And it wasn't a happy one. As we got to within ten feet of my beautiful car, I gasped in absolute horror! Every bird in town had taken a crap on my car… and the hot, sizzling sun had baked it on!!! All my hours of hard work had gone for naught! And I had to endure the chuckling and amusement of my coworkers! I was absolutely <u>Peeved</u>! There was no aggression. No consequences. But so much frustration and disappointment put me solidly in the "Peeved" zone. This time probably a 6 on the scale.

Watch out for the "Pissed Off" Zone. Herein lies that dangerous border area in which our primary triggers to Anger may be most easily identified. We are still safe here because we have not crossed over the line to "Enraged" where those of us with Anger issues are most vulnerable. In the "Enraged" Zone, or peak-of-the-pyramid, the targets of our wrath may get verbally attacked and threatened by us with bodily harm. In the "Enraged" zone people get clobbered, dishes get thrown, threats of destruction are made and people have their heads handed to them, perhaps after we knock their teeth down their throats!

But this is not that place. This is the "Pissed Off" zone where many of our angriest, most caustic situations, triggers and responses reside. But they remain short of the danger zone… and thank goodness for that because our reactions here will at least not lead us toward the painful consequences of jail time, lost relationships, lost jobs and more!

My most memorable – or should I say forgettable – snapshot of me in the "Pissed Off" zone involves a story I often share with my

Anger Management group participants. I consider myself a pretty nice person overall. I hold the door open for little old ladies. I leave my outside light on for Halloween Trick or Treaters. I throw a couple of bucks in the basket at Church on Sunday. I've even been known to help a homeless person with a buck or two.

One thing that REALLY "Pisses" me off though is when I have a verbal or handshake agreement with someone and they just act like it never happened! They proceed to do exactly whatever the hell they want, with total disregard and disrespect for my feelings and well being.

Such a situation arose recently when the kindly 92 year old lady who had lived above my ground floor apartment for five years was suddenly moved into a nursing home by her family. For the past six months, her apartment had been vacant. She never made much noise anyway but I had truly enjoyed the tomblike solitude and silence of having an empty apartment above me.

Of course I just knew that wasn't going to last forever. One day, as I was returning home from my office, the real estate guy who was seeking to rent out that upstairs apartment, approached me at my front door. "Good evening Mr. Haviland!" he exclaimed cheerfully. "I'd like to introduce you to the new tenants for that upstairs vacancy."

I turned to see a handsome young couple in their late twenties, standing in front of me. They seemed like a respectful, well dressed considerate young man and woman and I reached out my hand to greet them. "Welcome to the neighborhood," I said cheerfully. "This is a great community to live in. Plus you get a bonus – if you ever need a cup of sugar or milk, I'm right downstairs!" They chuckled and told me they planned to move in soon.

For the first three weeks, they were quieter than the old lady for God's sake. Every morning they were out the door by 7:30 am to go to work. That was a half hour earlier than my own departure time for the hospital where I was working at the time. And evenings were so quiet I wasn't even sure whether they owned a TV or a radio!

Then it happened. The event that ultimately sent me into the "Pissed" zone and ever so close to an act of verbal or physical aggression in the "Enraged" zone.

At first it seemed like just another Saturday night. I was sitting quietly in my downstairs apartment at about 7:30 pm, watching TV when all of a sudden my attention was drawn to the sidewalk outside my living room window. There droves of well dressed young people in their twenties and thirties began arriving on the scene, climbing the stairs to the upstairs apartment.

At about 8 pm the dance music starting blaring from every window and the ceiling above my humble abode began creaking and cracking as some 20 to 30 partiers began to dance the night away. And they danced, and partied, and danced some more. Hey, I said to myself, I was young once too. "Let the young people enjoy their Saturday night," I thought. I was pretty much OK with it all. Until, that is, the chandelier hanging above my bed began to rattle and shake, appearing that it just might break free of its fixture above me! My head started pounding. And then, on top of it all, it seemed they were never going to leave!

As my clock turned to midnight… then to 1 am… then to 2 am… then to 3 am, I lay sleepless in my bed, nursing a throbbing headache, and cursing the loud music and revelry above me, wondering how in hell I was going to get up at 6 am that morning and go to work! You see I was assigned to the ER at the hospital on Sundays and I had to be up there at 7 am to start my shift. As I struggled to catch even a little bit of shuteye, I vowed to have a talk with that young couple the following day. No question about that!

Everything seemed great as my new upstairs neighbors were falling all over themselves, apologizing profusely and promising to end their next party "no later than 12 midnight." Being the nice guy that I am, I told them that even 12:30 or 1 am would be fine. But they insisted: No later than 12 midnight!

Snuggling into bed the following Saturday night, I rested assured that all would go well. After all, I had the young couple's word, right? I wound up my bedside alarm clock and waited for the clock to strike 12 midnight when any second, I just knew that the party goers would be shuffling down the stairs, into their cars and off into the night. Yeah, hope springs eternal. But not on this night.

As the clock turned 1 am... then 2 am... then 3 am, the Anger within me seethed. Had the couple completely forgotten or disregarded the promise they had made to me?? I was "Pissed!" Throwing on my bathrobe and slippers I raced for the door... and literally leapt up the stairs until I found myself facing the young couple's door. "Bam, bam, bam" I pounded on the door, my rage and fury now reaching a fever pitch.

Suddenly the door flew open. "Whaaat??!!" the young male half of the couple bellowed in a highly perturbed manner, looking stoned, drunk or a combination of both.

Now it's important to recognize that I didn't grab him by the shirt and threaten to knock his teeth down his throat. I didn't push past him into the apartment, picking up his stereo and hurling it out the window, shattering it on the street below. And I didn't begin physically pushing his guests out the door, cursing at them as I muscled them down the stairs and out into the cold night air. I might have *imagined* doing these things. But any of these actions would have thrust me into the "Enraged" and Aggressive zone. Certain arrest and a trip to the local police precinct would have more than likely been my reward for any of those actions!

No, I was in control on this night. Er very early morning. Able to avoid physical and verbal aggression, I simply remained in the "Pissed" zone, and using my Assertiveness skills (which I will share with you soon enough) I merely looked him in the eye and said:

"Son, you have failed to live up to our simple agreement to end your party at a reasonable hour. It is now 3 am and once again I will fail to get a decent night's sleep before having to get up Sunday morning at 6 am to go to work. So here's the deal. The next time your party runs one minute after midnight, it won't be me you're seeing at your front door. You will get a painful visit from my friends in the local police department and you can deal with them. Have a nice day."

And I turned on my heel and headed back to my apartment downstairs. And yes. Having someone disrespectfully break a promise to me – especially when it affects my well being – can put me head over heels into the "Pissed" zone. In this particular case, with my rowdy, disrespectful upstairs neighbors pushing me to the limit, I hit a 9 on the scale.

And to be honest, my objective with this book is to help you with any specific Anger issue you may have to NEVER EXCEED THE PISSED OFF ZONE. Hopefully by recognizing your personal triggers and using the coping skills, cognitive restructuring and assertiveness training I will soon reveal… you will NEVER become physically or verbally aggressive. In fact, by monitoring your own Mindfulness Pyramid you will become more aware of those triggers that tick you off, peeve you or piss you off.

Hopefully their power over your emotions will slowly diminish. What once led you to the "Pissed Off" zone may even fall toward the "Peeved" or even the "Ticked Off" zones. You will begin to control your Anger and not vice versa! And you will recognize and short circuit those triggers BEFORE they burn you and those around you. And lead to the worst of consequences.

Next Up… A Trip To The "Enraged" (and Aggressive) zone with Yours Truly!

Better buckle your seat belt. What happens here is scary – both for the targets of our rage… but more importantly for you and me as that uncontrolled, unbridled rage leads to consequences that we cannot turn back from.

I am often reminded here of a situation in my life that could have easily become my worst nightmare. It's an episode in which my most vulnerable trigger – my impatience with people whom I have perceived as disrespectful of my time – rapidly climbed the Mindfulness Pyramid to sit firmly in the "Enraged" zone.

Everything started out innocently enough. It was a pleasantly warm Saturday morning in June. I had driven about 5 miles north of my home to pick up some light bulbs at a nearby hardware store. It was coming up on 11:30 am when I left the store and proceeded south enroute to my office near my home where I planned to meet with a patient at 12 noon.

Suddenly my hands-free phone on the dashboard began to blink, and I could see that my lovely wife was calling me from our home. I took the call. "Honey," she pleaded, "I am completely out of milk and bread. Could you stop at the supermarket on your way down and pick them up for me?" She continued to state her case: "I just know I won't get out in time to do it myself, with company coming later today and a whole house to clean before they come. Please do that for me? Pretty please?"

As she begged me in her cutest fashion, I couldn't help thinking how close I'd be cutting it timewise if I were to stop at the supermarket. Still, after arguing the issue back and forth, she somehow persuaded me to stop and I just hoped to get the milk and bread and then get to my 12 o'clock patient on time.

Despite my apprehension, things appeared to go pretty well from the start. I was able to grab a parking space close to the entrance door. And, knowing where the bread and milk were, I moved with cat-like speed through the aisles, grabbing both, and then made a beeline for the speedy "10 items or less" check out lines at the front of the supermarket.

Oops! My first problem. Both express lines were jam packed with customers. "Gee, of course!" I thought. "What the heck else would I expect at 11:40 on a Saturday morning??" My anxiety about missing my appointment was rising. That's when, to my delight, I saw that aisle 14 had only one customer in line. And that person, an elderly man, was reaching into his bag, perhaps to get his credit card to pay for the groceries that had already moved down the conveyor belt, ready to be bagged. The line even had a bagger ready to start putting the groceries in paper bags to move things along. Was this my lucky day?!

I ran up to the line and happily plunked my bread and milk down on the counter. Looks like I would make it to my 12 o'clock appointment after all! And that's when I heard the old man say the words that would soon rock my world: "I know that 5 cent coupon's in here somewhere."

In disbelief, and rapidly growing frustration, I turned my face toward the elderly man to make sure I had heard him correctly. The 80 something year old man simply smiled up at me and said it again: "I know that 5 cent coupon's in here somewhere."

My anger and frustration began to skyrocket up the Mindfulness Pyramid in leaps and bounds underscoring my primary trigger of impatience. What started in the "Peeved" zone since I was in an impatient rush to begin with… rapidly climbed toward the "Pissed Off" zone and points higher as I watched the elderly man take item after item out of his giant bag, meticulously placing each item on the counter.

"It's not in there," he chuckled as he placed an old, weathered wallet on the counter. "My sister gave me that wallet years ago, back in the nineteen fifties and I keep my Medicare cards in there," he sighed, reminiscing about those golden years. My heart raced as he proceeded to place a transistor radio, a 1964 World's Fair keychain, and an old movie ticket for The Godfather on the counter. I bit my lip and felt my face and neck flush the hottest shade of red. As I watched the elderly man examine each item he took out of his bag in his haphazard search for that elusive 5 cent coupon, I felt as though my head were about to explode.

I glanced entreatingly at the checkout girl as though, in my moment of soaring frustration, I thought that she could somehow, some way do something to turn this nightmarish situation around. But it took me only a second to realize that she had checked out long before, now just leaning up against the back of the register, smiling and exchanging text messages with her boyfriend. She was a million miles away.

As my Anger now soared to the top of the Pyramid scale, I glanced hopefully toward the young man bagging the groceries at the end of the counter. But guess what? He wasn't bagging at all! Rather he was crumpling up copies of the weekly supermarket circular, and shooting baskets like he was basketball All Star Steph Curry of the Golden State Warriors.

I looked at my watch and to my horror it was now almost a quarter to 12 noon and my chances of being on time for my patient were dwindling by the second. In this, my moment of total hopelessness and frustration, I wanted desperately to reach into my pocket for that nickel and three pennies worth of change I had stuffed in there earlier after buying a cup of coffee. And in my mind's eye, I imagined the unimaginable – I saw myself hurling the lousy eight cents change in his eighty year old face... while screaming at the top of my lungs: "Here's your goddamned 5 cent coupon! Now move your ass or I will move it for you!!"

The thought and height of my rage still sends chills through me from head to toe. Had I unleashed my flood of rage in a torrent of threats and expletives, I could only imagine the repercussions: Everyone in the store is suddenly looking my way with looks of terror and dread on their faces. They grab their groceries and hasten for the exit... while the Store Manager races to the scene, frantically speaking into his phone.

Who's he calling? How about the police? Not for the old guy holding up the line, searching for a 5 cent coupon. Not for the girl behind the register text messaging her boyfriend. And not for the kid shooting baskets instead of bagging. He's calling the police for ME!!!

And when they arrive, they will hastily slap me in handcuffs, push me toward the door like a common criminal, and likely stuff me into a squad car to be driven to the local precinct for fingerprinting and processing. I'll likely spend the night in jail and need to have my beloved wife come and bail me out. And the supermarket? They will likely get an order of protection against me preventing me from ever stepping into that store again. On top of it all, I was unable to meet with my 12 pm patient who was surely waiting for me in vain at my office!!

Consequences! Consequences! Consequences! That's what happens when we roar uncontrollably into that angriest realm of the Mindfulness Pyramid...the "Enraged" and Aggressive zone... a clear 10 on the scale... where physical or verbal aggression is our likely choice of action. Because we failed to address our primary trigger – in my case impatience – and blindly walked into that minefield of danger in which so many things conspire together to ensure our angriest and deadliest reactions to a situation.

My first mistake? Not recognizing at all times and being mindful of the fact that my most vulnerable trigger is IMPATIENCE!!! (Remember me waiting in frustration for that meatloaf to make its way around the table?) Walking into a crowded supermarket at one of the BUSIEST TIMES OF DAY! When I have the slimmest chance of shopping and still getting to a scheduled appointment on time under the absolute best of circumstances!! With the help of the Mindfulness Pyramid, I could have planned to avoid placing myself in harm's way. One former Supermarket Manager told me that after 9 pm the store is like a ghost town. I would always have the entire place to myself.

I have nobody to blame but myself. For not being mindful of my key trigger to Anger – Impatience – and for not monitoring it on the Mindfulness Pyramid. My Anger absolutely controlled me, and just like that volatile gas I talked about earlier, it exploded, leaving its carnage everywhere. Because I was not mindful, I walked into my worst possible minefield of destruction. And the carnage left behind was of my making. And the consequences would last a lifetime. Nasty.

CHAPTER 4

A GLANCE INTO ANGER'S BROKEN MIRROR

Ok. Now I've come clean on where <u>my</u> triggers are located on the Mindfulness Pyramid. From a simple "ugh" in the "Ticked Off" zone because I missed a green light… to a raging, aggressive "I want to grab you and trash you!" in the "Enraged" zone because someone in the Supermarket has stolen the time I needed to get to an important appointment. Because I am a human being just like you, I do manage to get perturbed by many of the things that happen to me in the process of my daily life. Missing green lights and getting stung by bees are not among my favorite things. But they will usually never exceed the "Ticked Off" zone for me and my reactions will not likely exceed a curse word or two. Even discovering that someone has eaten my mouthwatering roast beef sandwich at work is not likely to generate anything more than a childish tantrum in the "Peeved" zone. Neither will having my shiny new car crapped on by every bird in the neighborhood after I spent an entire day washing and waxing it! Sure I will be peeved. But nothing more than that. And you know what? Even having thoughtless, disrespectful neighbors rock and rolling over my head til 3:30 in the morning may get me into the "Pissed Off" zone. But it doesn't typically light the match toward an aggressive act that will end up with me in handcuffs and a rap sheet. No, for me, that is reserved for what I have recognized as my own Achilles heel.... MY IMPATIENCE! And until I began monitoring my impatience on the Mindfulness Pyramid, and seeing that it could truly reside in the "Enraged" and Aggressive Zone, I was fully at its mercy, likely to have one of those uncontrollable explosions at any time.

Yeah. The Mindfulness Pyramid has definitely helped me in avoiding those life shattering explosions that my impatience could ignite. And I'm grateful that I am able to monitor its ugly behavior through this device. But in the realm of anger, you and I need all the help we can get. Right? Especially when I know that in my case I have other triggers like being disrespected, being inconvenienced, and being lied to that can move rapidly toward the "Pissed Off" zone, and up to a rageful explosion if not monitored carefully enough. In my case, they may not be as instantly volatile for me as my impatience is. They may not move directly into the "Enraged" zone like my impatience typically does. But trust me, they're up there in the danger category. And they – as well as my primary trigger of impatience – can end up resulting in dire consequences if they hit that deadly mark of no return.

So that's where Anger's Broken Mirror can help. One of my own personal anger management exercises, "The Mirror" as I call it, works in conjunction with the Mindfulness Pyramid, to help me experience my rising anger firsthand as I teeter between the "Pissed Off" and "Enraged" zones.

And believe me, life can appear pretty damn ugly when I'm peering into that cracked mirror, seeing the grotesque reflection of myself at my angriest. There I am seething, raging, hissing with my emotions and actions about to boil over like hot, molten lava into my life.

I shudder to think of the consequences I might suffer. The Mindfulness Pyramid helps me monitor the intensity and levels of my anger. But it's looking into this personal Mirror that helps me witness a clear, snapshot-quality image of myself in that exact moment of teeth-clenching, fire-spitting, eye-popping anger as I head up the scale toward my moment of rage and the behavior that accompanies it. All to help me pull the plug on that burning toaster of fury and rage before the whole house burns down! And trust me, "The Mirror" can help you too when <u>awareness</u> of what you look like at your angriest moment combines with the <u>mindfulness</u> of your primary triggers and anger intensity to help you short circuit your anger before it gets the best of you.

Let me give you a glimpse at what I'm seeing in "The Mirror" on one particular occasion when my perception of being disrespected is pushed to the absolute brink: So I'm lying in bed on a Sunday morning, glad to be able to sleep in on my day off. It's early. Around 7 am. The weather report is for sunny skies and warm summery temperatures, and I'm thinking of how nice it would be to pack a picnic lunch and head out later with my wife and daughters to the park. But in the meantime, I'm just luxuriating in the calm and quiet of my lovely Sunday morning. Suddenly as I lay there drifting between a pleasant sleep and quiet relaxation... the deafening sound of lawn tractors, mowers, weed wackers, and other landscaping equipment rocks my once magical morning. My next door neighbor is having his lawn trimmed at 7 am on my one day off this week. Wow! Now, as I bound out of bed in a growing rage... Anger's Broken Mirror is about to reveal to me a self portrait of fury – which, if I can trust the Mirror and utilize it quickly enough – just might help me derail my anger before I do something that I'll regret. And avoiding the consequences of our actions is really what it's all about in the final analysis.

The Mirror shows it all! At first glance, my face and neck have become red hot, flushed and my heart is pounding a mile a minute. I'm breathing harder and faster by the second. Physically one glimpse into the imaginary Mirror shows that this sudden, inconsiderate intrusion onto my privacy and tranquility has turned a normally mild mannered, calm man into the Incredible Hulk. And what does the Mirror show about my behavior? I'm cursing my head off, threatening to call the police, the local Court, the President of the United States. Emotionally, I'm feeling disrespected, hurt and basically furious. And in my heart of hearts I want to head over to my neighbor's yard, knock on his door and punch him square in the face. Yes, by using Anger's Broken Mirror, I can see it all unfolding. But I can also make the decision to STOP. To end this action before I stumble into that personal minefield in the "Enraged" zone where I will truly suffer the consequences of my actions.

Being aware of that frighteningly scary image I project to other people as I am rising up the anger scale can help me. And it can help you too. In this case, one glimpse into Anger's Broken Mirror reminded me that red hot faces, cursing, feeling disrespected and wanting to punch someone in the face is not good. Since I don't want to go to jail or wage war against my next door neighbor and leave him bloodied and dead on his front lawn, the Mirror's ugly image enabled me to grab ahold of myself. I dropped the baseball bat, picked up the phone, and left a cordial but highly assertive voicemail for my neighbor letting him know that perhaps we could talk about the best times to cut our grass in the future.

Again, the "Mirror" enabled me to use my awareness of my personal anger traits or symptoms to sound the warning bell to STOP, pause and reconsider…just as the Mindfulness Pyramid enabled me to know that, based on past experience, feeling disrespected can easily put me in the "Enraged" zone, where I will pay with serious consequences.

Oh my God. I just recalled another crazy incident in which the "Mirror" literally saved me from myself and the terrible repercussions and consequences of unbridled rage. Tell me if this scenario would have put you into the "Pissed" zone almost immediately… and just inches from "Enraged" where throwing something or threatening someone would have been the least of your worries.

OK here goes. My therapist colleague and I decided to drive from our office to an upstate city – a rugged trip of almost 120 miles – in order to attend this 8 hour conference on the mental health benefits of Yoga (of all things). Now it's not that we, as psychotherapists, were genuine Yoga enthusiasts. Or that we simply couldn't wait to test our fragile back muscles by getting ourselves into pretzel poses like "downward dog." We were basically taking this course in order to satisfy the State Education Department's requirement for continuing education units, and this all day program was going to give us 7 and a half big ones. Not a bad haul since we are required to earn 36 credits over the course of three years.

Now this whole requirement that we need to earn so many units kind of puts me in the "Peeved" category right off the bat. First of all, this requirement didn't even exist five years ago. Somebody in an ivory tower came to the bright conclusion that professionals in my field don't learn enough just dealing every day with every possible mental health and relationship issue under the sun. Now we need to attend conferences and pay large sums of money just to keep our edge! So, interested in holding on to our professional licenses, my colleague and I shrugged our shoulders, plunked down our $199 each, got up at 5:30 in the morning and headed northward for a conference we hoped would be instructive and beneficial to us.

The trip up wasn't too bad. We both enjoyed talking shop, sharing war stories and throwing in some pro sports talk. It was a pleasant mix that helped us pass the time. Throughout the entire hour and a half we were on the road, however, I was focused on driving as rapidly as possible within the speed limit so that the two of us would get there on time.

Traffic was not a problem for most of the trip. But then as we came close to the hotel where the conference was being held, we hit a traffic jam that slowed us just a bit. We pulled into the parking lot at 8:30 am. Or exactly the time that the yoga conference was set to begin.

Now, since I wanted us to be on time, I had not asked to make a pit stop along the way. As I entered the hotel, my first thought was to hit the rest room… even before heading to the main ballroom where the conference was being held. My colleague waited for me, and the two of us arrived at the sign-in table outside the conference room at exactly 8:36 am. "You're late!" snarled the grouchy program assistant, an officious woman who clearly was miffed by the fact that we were tardy. She also scowled, "You're the only two men in the program." It was like she was saying, "After all, what do you expect from two men?!" In the manner of the old "hall monitors" I remember from Catholic grammar school, she used a severe, scolding tone and marked us both late on her paper… even though by my watch, six minutes late was not a monumental offense. Sheesh. The instructor had barely made it up to the podium.

Anyway, my colleague and I enjoyed the yoga sessions and actually learned some beneficial things along the way. After standing in place, breathing deeply and reaching for our chakras, we were given a lunch break at 12:30 and told to return in an hour to complete the program. My colleague and I enjoyed a delightful lunch at the hotel café, and he even paid for me since I had driven all the way up in my car. It was shaping up as a pretty pleasant occasion overall. Until we returned to the sign up table following lunch.

Now here's where the "Mirror" really helped me out. Without the ability to watch myself disintegrate in real time… watching my increasingly angry reflection in that mirror… I might clearly have entered the "Enraged" and Aggressive zone and ended up in jail that night.

So we get back from lunch, prepare to sign back in and the program assistant greets us with the following declaration: "The two of you will not be receiving your certificates for this program today because you were both late this morning. If you want the certificate and the 7 and a half continuing education units, you will have to appeal to the company at their headquarters."

Talk about a trigger. I felt like she had just delivered a knock out punch to the gut that sent me reeling. As my colleague and I looked on in shock, the woman wrote on a sheet that we had achieved only "Partial Participation in the Yoga Program" and were not to receive our certificate or our credits for the course.

As my colleague shrugged unhappily, resigned himself to a "lost day," and sauntered into the conference room for the rest of the conference... I stood my ground and felt the blood surging in my neck, face and hands. I was incredulous that this nasty person, who was clearly filled with an air of her own self importance, was about to deny us what we had come 120 miles for. And paid $199 each for! With the anger I felt at that moment, you could have cooked an egg on my forehead!

"You are actually going to punish us for being six minutes late?!" I demanded to know. "Are you kidding me???" "You were actually ten minutes late," she snarled back, her raspy voice rising 5 octaves. She proceeded to tell me how she had called the company office earlier and was informed by a clerk there that she had the power to mark us late, thereby preventing us from gaining any benefit whatsoever from the conference. In other words, we were just "shit out of luck."

The anger in me was surging out of every pore but knowing that I had the "Mirror" to watch myself and monitor my reaction, helped me big time. I was holding back the dam of a rageful tirade that easily could have put me in jail. In fact, I could visualize the City Swat Team descending upon the hotel, putting me in their rifle sights! I continued to question my tormentor: "So you are marking us late and saying that we had only "partial participation" in the conference because we were six minutes late?! In other words you are punishing me and my colleague because I made the decision to go to the bathroom before I arrived at the sign in table???" She simply shrugged and said something like "Those are the rules."

I demanded to have her name, and the phone number for the company. While I felt totally disrespected by this assistant, and could feel the physical and emotional repercussions of that perception churning inside me, I was not going to allow myself to "lose it" and hit the "Enraged" zone with consequences that I would forever regret. But over "my dead body" I vowed that I would not leave that conference without my certificate and my 7 and a half credits which I had paid nearly $200 for!

I resolved to call the headquarters and plead my case with them. As my head continued to spin during the entire afternoon session – essentially stealing all the value of what the instructor was saying from me – I left the conference room three times on the pretense of going to the restroom in order to make that phone call to the company. It was maddening as I called the number that was given to me only to be told by the robotic voice on the other end that they would "answer the call in the order in which it was received." And that put me at customer number 3 the first two times I phoned!!

Desperate as the conference was drawing to a close, I raced up to the Instructor – a Yoga expert from a foreign country – to ask her to intercede on our behalf in this very foolish and bizarre situation. But she waved me off, just as my colleague had predicted. My only shot now was to get through to the company headquarters before the assistant packed up her paperwork and headed out the door.

Suddenly, on the third try, I hit paydirt. "Hello, my Name Is Annie. How can I help you?" Stumbling over my words, I pleaded my case, telling Annie that this hard hearted assistant was going to deny us our credits and certificate just because we were 6 minutes late for the start of the conference… and that I was only late at all because I had just driven 120 miles and had to rush to the restroom as soon as I entered the hotel.

Annie was more than understanding. "I am so sorry that you had to go through this," she said. "Some of our meeting assistants have difficulty following the correct procedures, and I apologize deeply for that." Annie asked to speak to the assistant who at this point was livid that her little plan to deny us our hard earned certificates was about to be derailed. Now the assistant turned her wrath on Annie: "One of your very own fellow managers told me I was fully in my rights to mark them late, and deny them their certificates," she yelled into the receiver. But I could see from the look on her face, that this woman was not going to get her way. My colleague and I walked away with our completion certificates and our continuing education units. And because I was continually using my "Mirror" throughout this troubling experience to monitor the way I felt, the way I acted, and my emotions, I never flew headlong into the potential rage that simmered just below the surface.

Now it's YOUR TURN to glance into Anger's Broken Mirror and determine for yourself what you look like and what your own snapshot reveals – all in that dangerous moment when your anger is increasing to the point where <u>you</u> could reach that "Enraged" zone and suffer consequences that could change your life for the worst.

Just in case you haven't got a solid idea yet of your own Achilles heel, take a look at some of the triggers I've assembled below to see where you are likely to be the most vulnerable when the situation arises. Is it somebody cutting you off on a busy road? Is it someone borrowing your lawnmower and never returning it? Is it being put on hold while your entire lunch hour disappears? Or waiting an hour in the Doctor's Office? Only you know what can send you head over heels into the kind of unbridled, mind searing rage that blindsided me in the story of the old man with the 5 cent coupon.

Be honest. What ticks you off? What peeves you? What really pisses you off? And finally, what specific trigger or triggers can leave you shaking in your boots with bone shattering rage and aggression... setting you up for the kind of consequences that can turn your life upside down?

Check these triggers out just to get the juices flowing:

- A grouchy spouse snarling at you after you've worked all day
- Somebody not returning your drill or wheelbarrow
- Waiting over an hour at the Doctor's office
- Somebody accusing you of something you didn't do
- Someone flat out lying to you
- A person driving 20 miles per hour in a 45 mph zone
- A snotty waitress providing crappy service
- Neighbors playing loud music at 2 am
- A colleague leaving extra work for you to do
- Being cut off on the road and almost getting into a crash
- Having your property vandalized or stolen
- Being given the wrong directions

Take the time to think about your appearance and thoughts as you deal with the triggers that make you most likely to soar up into the "Enraged" zone on the pyramid. One glimpse into Anger's Broken Mirror can help you avoid the violent reactions that could truly lead to consequences like jailtime, loss of job and loss of relationship.

Now let's try to grab ahold of the angriest, most rageful situation you've ever endured and step onto the "Stage of Rage!" You're about to get a clear and ugly look into the mirror at yourself at that moment right before the match is lit. Right before the physical threats. Right before the physical aggression.

You're about to see the reflection of that "Jeckyl & Hyde" character that you are, so nice so much of the time. But capable of unspeakable anger and rage that can set the world on its end! As you peer into that broken mirror, be sure to notice the entire picture of that "Angry You" as you soar upward through the Mindfulness Pyramid. Let this experience inform you, guide you and help you gauge where your weakest spots are. So that you can finally have that "Aha" moment where your trigger and the resulting anger will never control you again in the "Enraged" zone. Rather, because of your mindfulness, you will be in control, and that will make all the difference.

In my Anger Management groups, I always invite the participants to imagine themselves standing up on that "Stage of Rage," engaged in a raging conflict, teetering on the edge of flipping out., and fast heading toward the "Enraged" zone. I ask each person to step outside themselves, like an "out of body" experience, and walk across the stage, down the steps and over to the front row of our imaginary theater. Sitting with me in that front row, the two of us can now look up at themselves, caught up in that explosive moment with the target of their anger. Watching as the drama unfolds to catch each nuance and characteristic we see in ourselves at that exact moment.

For the sake of conversation, and to get you started, let's use a specific pretend scenario that many of us married or dating folks are familiar with: That quite unpleasant incident during which one person accuses the other of spending too much money, failing to help with the chores around the house, drinking or smoking too much, or — God forbid – having the gall to cheat on us with someone else, shaking our feeble sense of security in the relationship. Watch and recall how that particular confrontation with your partner might play out right up there on the stage.

Pretend you've just returned from work at the end of the day. You're tired, hungry, and all you'd like from your loved one is a pat on the back, a hug and the comforting words that "everything's going to be all right." But on this particular occasion, you've just seen a suspicious truck leaving the driveway as you pull up. A million questions flood your mind. Could your significant other be messing around with the plumber or the cable guy while you're out busting your ass for your family? Is he or she cheating on you while you're out killing yourself?

Now the snapshot of you being triggered, this time by feelings of jealousy and deception, is beginning to come into focus. You are rapidly climbing the anger scale in the Mindfulness Pyramid. You discover that infidelity is high on your personal anger scale. In fact it can easily reside within your "Enraged" and Aggressive zone. As you approach your significant other, you feel that distinct loss of control. You are judge, jury and executioner. You step forward with words that are accusatory, rageful, condemning…

It is at this exact moment that Anger's Broken Mirror can reveal you as you truly are. What does the Mirror say about how are you feeling right about now? Is your blood pressure surging… are you feeling flushed, hot in your cheeks or neck? Maybe you feel tension in your neck and shoulders. Or maybe your heart is pumping like never before. That adrenaline rush is a clear sign that you may be racing up toward the "Enraged" aggressive zone of the Mindfulness Pyramid. Noticing the rapid movement toward rage, what else is happening to you? Some people get clammy hands, watery eyes and dry mouth. Others get headaches or stomach aches as they soar up the anger scale. It's important to witness your own physical traits so that you can monitor how fast you're going up the Mindfulness Pyramid, and pull the plug on that "burning toaster" before we threaten someone or physically clobber them over the head. That's when we end up with consequences that are worse than the problem we're arguing about!

We can see how we feel physically as we look up on that Stage of Rage. But what are you doing right about now? Some people just stare quietly when they get angry. But if you're like me, almost the opposite is true. As I go up the scale (like during that situation at the supermarket with the old guy with the 5 cent coupon), I can be cursing, swearing under my breath, gesturing with my arms. Just know that if you and I start throwing furniture, grabbing our significant other's phone and tossing it in the toilet, punching holes in the wall, or crashing our car into their car…we have definitely hit the "Enraged" aggressive zone. Do anything close to those actions and we will be suffering consequences like jail, lost jobs, broken relationships. You get the idea.

And what are we feeling up on that stage? If infidelity, for example, is a primary trigger for you – and I can't imagine it wouldn't be for anyone – you're likely feeling jealous, hurt and disrespected in a big way. All of those can be fueling the anger you feel inside. This is where we can choose to see where our trigger resides – heading for the "Enraged" zone – and catch ourselves before we become destructive. Explosive. Violent. Physically or verbally. But the only way we can steer clear of the "Enraged" zone, given the tendency of our worst triggers to come upon us in explosive style, without warning, is to recognize it – and control it – before it is too late. That takes practice and that's exactly what looking in Anger's Broken Mirror, and using the Mindfulness Pyramid, can achieve for us!

Finally, what does the "Mirror" reveal about what you're thinking? You could simply be shaking your head, wondering how you got yourself into this mess. Or you could be rapidly planning to physically attack the person who has upset you. Watching these ugly thoughts floating through your consciousness in the "Mirror" will give you the opportunity to stand outside yourself and say, "I will not allow myself to reach this level 10 in the "Enraged" zone. The "Mirror" serves as your warning bell and it can make all the difference for you and your life.

Spend a few minutes looking into the "Mirror" and tell me what you see. Physically, Behaviorally, Emotionally and Mentally you are about to get a straight on view of yourself at your angriest. That view – like the Mindfulness Pyramid – will give you another tool by which you can become more aware of YOUR specific triggers, habits and attitudes… and ultimately help you short circuit your anger before you hit that "Enraged" zone of tragic consequences.

CHAPTER 5

PULLING THE PLUG ON ANGER

OK. We are getting closer to recognizing and controlling key aspects of our own personal Anger problems. That awareness through the Mindfulness Pyramid and Anger's Broken Mirror is invaluable in our quest to win this battle. We are essentially removing the blinders we've worn all these years… and we are staring the Beast right in the face. In all its gruesome, demonic, mind-searing reality. This is a huge step toward controlling our Anger versus our past experience of being controlled by our Anger. But seeing our triggers and behaviors in broad daylight is only part of the freaking job! Without skills that can pull us away from the impending crash… we may still dive headlong into that catastrophic moment of self destruction.

That's where we can use some real life tools, skills and strategies to short circuit the impulses that are surging within us. I'm not talking about holding your breath and counting to 100… hiding in a dark closet… or moving to a remote monastery where you can live out your life in self imposed solitude and separation from all other living human beings. As attractive as these options might sometimes feel, it isn't really practical for folks like us who do get some satisfaction out of living in the real world. There are ways to control our anger and still enjoy all the good things life has to offer, like job success, happy family life and the fruits of our hard work and determination.

One of the best ways I can think of to accomplish the task of pulling the plug on anger – especially in that frighteningly overwhelming moment when it threatens to derail everything good in our lives – is taking a Time Out. No, I'm not referring here to that old grammar school memory of finding ourselves sitting in the corner because we just put bubble gum in the hair of the kid sitting in front of us. Or even that basketball moment when we're down by a bucket with one second left to play and all we've got is a prayer of tying up the game. I'm talking about a truly effective adult Time Out when – after being cunningly aware of what's happening to us via the Mindfulness Pyramid, and gazing into Anger's Broken Mirror, we stare our worst impulses in the eyes… and decide NOT to allow our Anger to control us! We actually look into the eyes of the person we'd like to strangle, cripple and maim and say "I'm calling a Time Out."

Sure, you're probably thinking "what a juvenile, knuckleheaded thing to do." But you know what? You'd be WRONG because once you get into the habit of using this simple but amazingly effective tool, you will never again fall victim to that instant explosion of blinding fury. Why? Because YOU will be controlling your anger, and not the other way around!

In explaining the power of the Time Out in my anger management sessions, I often share a slightly funny, but potentially disastrous, situation in which a spouse (in this case me) returns home after a long day's work and takes issue with the way my wife is feeding our youngest child. So here goes…

I've just arrived home after a tough day at the office. Several cancellations. The air conditioning crapped out. And I misplaced some important paperwork. Great. Just another typical day. But now I'm pulling into the driveway at home, and thoughts of sitting in front of the fireplace, and kicking back with a glass of wine and some pleasant conversation with my lovely wife Debbie fill my tired head. I open the front door and flash a tired smile toward my wife who is sitting at the kitchen table with our young daughters Stephanie and Rebecca. Actually, our younger, one year old daughter Becca is in a high chair pulled up very close to where my wife is seated. And that's when I notice something that puts me immediately in the "Ticked Off" zone. My lovely wife is feeding our daughter Pizza Squares! Those horrible, frozen treats from the local Big Box Store that are loaded with preservatives, saturated fat and monosodium glutamate – to my mind, absolute poison for our darling little daughter who is lapping them up, stuffing them in her mouth and delighting in getting pizza sauce all over herself and her high chair.

And that's when, in my state of frustration and tiredness, I say the words that are about to cause my day to take a definite turn for the worse: "Gee, sweetheart, you think maybe we should be feeding Becca more nutritious foods? You know, like fruits, veggies and yogurt?"

Now, I never meant to be mean-spirited or hyper critical. Gosh it was just an observation for God's sake. And 10% of the time, a spouse might look at the box, read the ingredients, and say "Wow, hon. I never realized how much crap is in these pizza squares. You are right dear!" But more likely, 90% of the time, a spouse will look up from the table and say "OK smart ass. So what makes you Doctor Oz all of a sudden???!!!!"

And that's exactly what my lovely wife does. "As I recall," she sneers over her condescending smirk, "Your Mom wasn't even home to feed you. She was out working all day." And that's when she starts slinging the mud in my direction: "I seem to remember you saying that you and your little brother barely survived on white bread and jelly sandwiches for dinner!"

And that's when I – now not able to stop myself — reach into my pockets to sling some mud back at HER! "Are you kidding???"

I scream. "Since your lazy ass Mother was lying in bed all day, you and your little brother survived on microwave popcorn and a glass of water!" And then she dug deep and slung some more mud back at me: "Yeah? Nobody was as bad as your stupid ass brother. When Becca's at his place, he feeds her nothing but the cheapest hot dogs and beans. I'm surprised she doesn't come home sick whenever she visits him." Now the battle is in full force and we are both rapidly rising up the Mindfulness Pyramid, and I can't help slinging more mud back at my wife. "Sick???" I yell, with my face getting redder by the second, and blood vessels bulging in my neck. "You talk about sick??? How about every time Becca visits your insane sister who insists on feeding her nothing but ice cream and M&M's? I thought I'd have to take our poor daughter to the Emergency Room last time I picked her up over there!!!"

Now this is where, with neither party willing to back down or give in, really bad things can start happening. Once two people are unable to control their Anger, (failing to even use the Mindfulness Pyramid or The Mirror to at least witness their Anger rising) a lock-down, hell-bent ego battle rages forward. Coffee cups and dinner plates start flying across the room. Furniture gets smashed. Threats are made. A neighbor may call the police. And our cute little daughter Becca? Before she starts crying her eyes out, she's looking up at me and then looking up at her Mom and she's thinking to herself "But I thought this conversation was about me!!!"

Yes the conversation started out being completely about our daughter whom both my wife and I love dearly. But because of the perceived disrespect tearing into each of us, it was not long before our triggers were ignited. And the angry confrontation became more about ridiculously preserving our individual self respect than it was about doing the right thing for our daughter.

Left unchecked, the fruits of our inability to control our Anger would have been catastrophic. We'd both be led out in handcuffs… and our daughter shuttled off to a foster home. How ugly are those consequences??!!

Luckily there is a way to pull the plug on this horrible scene. It's the simple, straightforward Time Out. Now let's rewind this scenario back to a still manageable moment when I was faced with a choice: I could engage fully with my wife's mud slinging attack after the first salvo, return fire, and suffer the disastrous consequences of that action as described above. OR recognize via my knowledge of the Mindfulness Pyramid that being humiliated and ridiculed by my wife (or anyone for that matter) is one of the triggers that can rapidly send me personally into the "Enraged" zone. Knowing that, and using Anger's Broken Mirror to monitor the nasty changes occurring to me physically and behaviorally, I am now choosing to step away. Yank the plug on this flaming disaster of a moment. And avoid the consequences that surely would have come my way. After her first words of attack, I say...

"Hon, are you going to be here say 45 minutes from now?" She barks back at me, "Sure, where the hell am I going to go? I'm here with the kids aren't I???" I respond matter-of-factly. "Sure, well I'm going to take a Time Out. I have to get some stamps at the Post Office and I also have to go to the supermarket to pick up a few things. But I should be back in about 45 minutes." She growls at me from her seat at the kitchen table but I continue. "When I come back I'd like to make you a cup of tea. And then maybe we can go on line, check out Web Md, or some other sites and learn something about the best foods to feed our little Becca."

As I'm walking out the door, I remind my wife that I never said she was a "bad mother." In fact, I praised her for the wonderful things she always does for me and our little family. With that, I leave the house and head for the Post Office and the supermarket. I have done one of the most powerful things possible to avoid the consequences of Anger. I have taken a Time Out.

Now fast forward 45 minutes. I've got my stamps. Picked up the groceries. I'm heading back home in my car, but I can't, for the life of me, remember what I'm supposed to focus on upon my return.

Finally it dawns on me. Oh yes! The pizza squares! I have to speak with my wife about that nutrition issue!

Now when I arrive at the front door, she just might possibly meet me with the pizza squares box in her hands, with a look of disbelief on her face. "I can't believe the ingredients in this stuff," she might say. "Gosh, the saturated fat alone is through the roof!" More likely she will meet me at the front door with her arms folded, remaining skeptical of my opinions on nutrition, challenging me to show her how we can improve the way we feed our daughter.

The bottom line is this. Before I left the house on my Time Out, we were allowing our anger to control us. And likely it would not have been long before we both reached the "Enraged" zone of the Mindfulness Pyramid. God knows you could see how rapidly we moved up the scale as we slung mud at each other, both standing our ground and refusing to pull the plug on our anger. But in the scenario where I leave the house and come back to discuss the source of our frustration 45 minutes later… we are both likely to be calmer, less stressed, less angry overall. And we'd likely be able to measure our Anger somewhere in the "Peeved" zone. Because lowering blood pressure – and the likelihood of serious consequences – is what taking a Time Out is all about! Try it.

For many people, breathing exercises serve as another way to lower the level of our Anger in that moment when inaction can lead to deadly fury and rage. I know that many counselors and therapists do at least give lip service to the idea of using breathing exercises to calm oneself down during emotional crises. And these crises can range from full blown anxiety and panic attacks to escalating anger, moving rapidly on its way toward rage. The bottom line is that the function of breathing in specific, metered ways appears to help us regain control of ourselves because of the physiological impact it has on us as human beings.

I read a pretty interesting article in one of the New York area newspapers over a year ago which brought into sharp focus a very different, yet powerful, use of breathing as a coping skill in meditation form. Turns out that a group of Army veterans had just returned from active duty in Afghanistan and were seeking mental health assistance from their Veterans Administration Office in order to treat the typical emotional ravages of life in the battle zone. Most of the soldiers, all of whom were male in this particular group, were struggling with Post Traumatic Stress Disorder, a common mental health issue among returning veterans. In some cases, the problem was so acute that a sudden, loud noise could send the afflicted soldier into a tailspin of emotional upheaval. Other symptoms were sleeplessness and extreme vigilance which proved both exhausting and crippling emotionally.

In their search for relief, they came to The VA with expectations that they would participate in group and individual therapy, while perhaps taking some medications that might be prescribed for them. Well imagine the men's surprise when the head psychiatrist advised them that they would also be participating in yoga and breathing meditation as part of their treatment! Their initial overall response? "You're not going to put us in tights and have us chanting Om on some God forsaken yoga mat!!" The Psychiatrist's reaction was swift and unequivocal: "If you are going to participate in my mental health program, you will definitely be doing meditation and yoga." After a brief, yet heavy silence the soldiers reluctantly agreed to participate in the psychiatrist's program – yoga, meditation and all.

Following six weeks of treatment, the soldiers agreed to a man – nothing they had ever experienced before, had provided as much relief as that meditation! Having incorporated the breathing meditation into my Anger Management Program proved to be an effective and powerful tool enabling participants to short circuit their anger, just as the soldiers had used it to help them control their PTSD and general anxiety. And the technique couldn't be simpler. JUST LISTEN TO YOUR BREATH coming in and out of your nose.

Here's how I recommend you do it, just as I recommend it to my group participants:

Simply find a comfortable, quiet place to sit – somewhere you won't be disturbed by extraneous sounds like ringing phones, loud music, or traffic noise – close your eyes and simply listen to your breath coming in and out of your nose. It's that simple! Personally, I just sit there and focus my full attention on the sound of my breath coming in and out of nose, imagining my closed eyes focused downward toward my nose, while my ears listen intently to the soft sound of each breath gliding in and out of my nostrils. I typically invite my anger management group participants to join me in this little exercise, and we will sit together just listening to our breath for a minute or so. Even in that short a time, folks will exclaim that they feel calmer, more emotionally under-control, even achieving a near trance-like tranquility which pulls the plug on any feelings of rage, frustration, angst or seething anger that may have controlled them just seconds before.

While this is the simplest kind of meditation you'll ever hear about, its power over the emotions that control us – from PTSD to Anger – is unmistakable. Try it after a long, busy day of dealing with frustrating bosses, customers and family members. It will have an other-worldly effect, transporting you from a place of anger to one of inner peace. Or use it when you awaken to set the stage for a calm, tranquil day where those typical triggers can't derail you. You'll be amazed at the power of this breathing meditation in your life… just as the soldiers returning from Afghanistan did. You can believe it!

Another, more traditional, breathing exercise that can build peace and tranquility… and which I highly recommend… has everything to do with bringing oxygen into your lungs, holding it for a count of seven, and ultimately expelling it for a count of eight, compressing your lungs as hard as you can. Imagine just sitting straight up in a comfortable chair, and breathing in through your nose as powerfully as you can. Fill those lungs with oxygen! And now, at the height of your inbreath, count slowly to seven as you hold the oxygen deep in your lungs. One... two... three... four... five... six... seven. Now are you ready to exhale? Do so through your mouth, this time counting slowly to eight until you have released every molecule of breath from your body. Your diaphragm should almost ache as you seek to pressure every ounce of breath out of you. Prepare to do this several times and notice the sense of peace and awareness that come over you. This is the kind of exercise that can help keep you on an even keel... almost like a preventative technique, that keeps you grounded and less vulnerable to your angry tendencies. It's fine as an everyday technique to retain that sense of overall calm. But as a breathing exercise to help you pull the plug at the moment of rising anger? Maybe not so great.

I wondered what it would take in terms of a breathing exercise that I could give participants in my anger management groups to really alter or effect the level of their anger. This last technique was not the answer. But based on my own past experience, I did actually have a breathing technique that could fit the bill. A technique that in my moment of greatest emotionality, and loss of control, would come to my rescue. Extinguish my rising Anger. Nip my emotionality in the bud. And it came to me in a very unusual way – through a personal experience that I will never forget.

Turn the clock back a few years. After running several of my anger management groups on a rainy Saturday afternoon in March, I had agreed to see a 37 year old woman whom I had been counseling for several years. On this particular Saturday, she entered my office wringing her hands with a worried look etched on her face. She was teary eyed, and started weeping openly. After passing her a box of tissues, I sat back in my chair, and then leaned forward: "I'm sorry. Please tell me what has got you so upset?" I asked in as compassionate a voice as I could muster. After settling down, she gave me the answer I looked for. "It looks like I am never going to have my ten year old son and my nine year old daughter back in my life again," she moaned, dabbing her eyes with the tissues I had given her. She went on to tell me the whole painful story, much of which I already knew. She stated that after two whole years of fighting her wealthy ex husband in court for partial custody of her son and daughter, she was about to throw in the towel. In fact with just one more Court appearance scheduled, her attorney had basically told her that their case was "unwinnable" and that now – in the eleventh hour – maybe I, as this woman's therapist, would be willing to step forward and testify in Court on her behalf. From her attorney's perspective, it was a last ditch attempt to turn things around after months and months of Court appearances and failed attempts to win partial custody of her children.

On the surface, one would wonder how, in God's name, this woman could ever lose custody of her kids in the first place. Despite being divorced, at 37 she was a highly trained medical technician who was well paid and had the ability to provide very well for herself. She was also a dedicated member of the community who was known and appreciated for her work with local charities and her church. She had a lovely home, and really wanted for nothing. By my description, you'd be hard pressed to imagine this woman ever on the losing end in Court in a case regarding her two children. But the fact is, things weren't always this way.

Ten years ago, this fine woman was actually a fall-down-on-your face drug addict, living in a hovel of an apartment somewhere in the south Bronx. Not one of New York's flashiest communities at the time. On one dismal day, as she lay prone and unconscious on the living room floor, her son and daughter – then 2 and 1 year old respectively – scratched and foraged for something to eat, tearing into a bag of cereal they managed to find in the kitchen. As that sad scene unfolded, there came a knock on the door. It was her ex husband and in his hands he carried papers from his attorney. "Look," he said to her, "Sign the papers and turn full custody of the kids over to me. You can't possibly care for them in your condition, not even for a weekend visit. Just look at you! When you're back on your feet, I'll work something out. At least that will be better than having some neighbor seeing you like this, and calling the cops and CPS."

My patient, knowing full well the severity of her predicament, decided she had no alternative. She signed the papers. Her ex husband then whisked the two children off in his limousine to his country estate. Over the passing years, he made sure they were well taken care of, with a top education, trips to foreign countries, and the best life that money could buy.

Ultimately my patient turned her life around, determined to get her kids back and convinced that she could finally be the mother her children deserved. After years in recovery, she spoke to her wealthy ex husband about sharing custody of the children again, as he had initially promised to do. But he would have none of it. When she called his home to speak to the kids, he hung up the phone, time and time again. When she realized that only legal action could help her regain partial custody of the children, she sought a decision in Court. At the Court's request, she even went for hair follicle testing – the most definitive proof that she was now drug and alcohol free. And she tested negative again and again!

But her ex husband dug in his heels. Hiring the highest priced attorney in all of the Midwest, he fought her for nearly two years to retain full custody of the children. Maintaining that she was a lifelong drug addict who would always be a danger to the children. And now, with only one Court appearance left, it looked like her quest to have their children back in her life was all but over.

My heart went out to her as I watched her continue to sob as she recounted the story. "My attorney feels that if you would testify on my behalf, it might turn the tide," she whispered.

Now I had never testified in Court before. And I had no desire to do it now. "Winning this case is really your attorney's responsibility," I argued. "I'm sorry. I really wish I could help, but I doubt that my appearance would make a difference."

As my patient left my office that rainy day, I felt really bad for her. And that night I couldn't sleep, going over and over in my mind how callous her ex husband seemed to be. What really got to me was how heartless he appeared, hanging up the phone when she called, not even allowing the children to speak to their own mother who loved them so much. The more I thought about this, the angrier I became, and by morning I was solidly lodged in the "Pissed Off" zone of the Mindfulness Pyramid. I decided to act. I called my patient. "I will testify," I said.

I wouldn't hear from the Court for another week or so. When they did call, they gave me a time and date to appear. And my Anger against my patient's ex husband was sizzling.

On the day I was due to testify, I arrived at the Court about an hour early. Peering into what I thought was the main courtroom, I settled my nerves with the thought that the scene didn't look too daunting or too challenging. Just a small courtroom. I'll appear for a moment or two. And then I'll be done. It couldn't have been further from the truth.

A court official noticed me looking around, and then straightened me out. "No, this is not the Courtroom," he stated. "This is the Courtroom," he said, slowly pulling open two huge doors that reminded me more of the giant iron doors at Saint Patrick's Cathedral in New York than what I'd expect to see at the entrance way to a Courtroom. As I peeked inside, the image that met my eyes was absolutely mind boggling. There, sitting at least 20 feet high on a huge platform was His Honor, the Judge. Below him, at least eight to ten of his minions sat… typing, processing paperwork, making phone calls. Way below where they sat, the ex husband and his high priced attorney plotted their legal strategy, while on the other side of the ground floor, my patient sat with her grim faced attorney, hoping for a miracle that would return her two children to her through partial custody.

"That's right," said the court official. "This is the Courtroom. Now you go back and sit in that little room outside until the Judge calls for you to testify."

And that's where I went. And I sat, and sat, and sat some more. Waiting for the Judge's call. Suddenly, as I waited in that little room, my initial Anger toward the ex husband for his callous, insensitive attitude toward my patient… began turning into something quite different.

As I realized that this was perhaps her last opportunity to get partial custody of her kids, I became apprehensive, even anxious. As I thought of how I needed to hit a genuine home run with my testimony, my anxiety soared. And I now alternated between feeling angry and anxious. My emotional state became so volatile that I tried every breathing exercise I knew to calm myself down. First I tried the meditative breathing, where I quietly sought to listen to my breath naturally coming in and out of my nose… hoping that this would provide some relief. But after a few minutes, I realized that this was neither the time nor the place for that form of breathing.

I quickly changed gears and began to do the exercise where I would breathe in deeply through my nose, hold my breath for a count of seven… then exhale through my mouth for a count of eight. I did several rounds of this breathing exercise and felt some relief, but once again my jumbled emotions of anger, anxiety and apprehension proved too powerful. I leaped out of my seat in desperation. Unable to control my emotions, I feared the worst – that I would be terribly shaky, nervous and apprehensive on the stand. And that would spell doom for my patient's hopes to see her son and daughter again.

That's when a thought of brilliant enlightenment popped into my head. I recalled a different kind of breathing exercise that I had witnessed while watching athletes at the recent Olympic Games prepare for their events. Specifically, I remembered athletes on the high dive board, breathing in and out in an extremely rapid cadence. In through the nose, out through the mouth. So rapidly and powerfully in and out, that if they were to do 20 or more of these in rapid succession – according to a nurse friend of mine – they would keel over and faint right then and there. I began to do the breathing exercise as though my life depended on it. Amazingly, the results helped me quell my weird, debilitating concoction of emotions. (In my Anger Management sessions, I invite my participants to join me in this breathing exercise. I always ask if they are smokers first, because the powerful process of sucking in air through the nose and blowing it out through the mouth requires good lung capacity. And I certainly don't want anyone to keel over from over oxygenation!)

Anyway, back to my pre-testimony dilemma. As I sat there breathing in and out at an ultra fast pace, I felt the apprehension, anger and anxiety that controlled me magically lifting. In its place (probably because of the deep oxygenation of my brain) I felt a strange, calming sense of serenity. Suddenly all the tension was gone. I felt almost "high" as I held my unshaking hands out in front of me. And that's when the Judge called me into the Courtroom.

As I walked into the huge Courtroom, and began the climb up the stairway toward the Judge, I remember calmly, confidently saying to myself "I've got this! I am soooo calm. I am so ready to testify and I have no fear."

The Judge directed me to put my right hand on the Bible. "You swear to tell the truth, the whole truth and nothing but the truth? So help you God?" he asked. I responded crisply and clearly: "I do." The Judge then asked me a few questions regarding my patient and what I knew of the case. No stress. I answered his questions fully. The attorney for my patient then threw me a few "home run ball" questions that I could knock out of the park. And I proceeded to do so.

And then the attorney from Hell – the ex husband's high priced lawyer who was putting his son through college with the money he was making from this case alone — came at me with his very best shot. "You are unprofessional!" he growled, yelling so loudly that everyone in the courtroom and beyond could hear him. "You failed to contact the children's psychiatrist, and you failed to contact the counselor who their father has been seeing. You don't know anything about the case or the people involved. You are unprofessional!"

Now, had I *not* done those rapid fire breathing exercises before heading to the stand, there is no doubt that the attorney's harangue would have rattled me. In fact I would likely have been shaking so badly, that I would have stuttered something like "I guess, I guess maybe I should have. I'm, I'm not sure." But not on this day. Because I was in control of all my emotions – and, to be sure, Anger and Anxiety are close cousins when it comes to the power they can wield over us and how uncontrollable they can both be. But I was so calm after those breathing exercises that I simply looked the attorney in the eye and replied: "Actually, I didn't have to. You see I have been treating the children's mother as my patient in therapy for nearly two years now, so I didn't have to contact anyone else."

I went on to say that my patient, a 37 year old professional woman, was doing very well now. That she had a high paying job at a local hospital. And that she was involved with the local Church group. She had a lovely home in the area and was financially independent. And totally committed to being a good mother to her kids. At that point I turned and looked up at the Judge to make another important point. "And as you know Your Honor, my patient has gone through two rounds of hair follicle testing. And she has come up negative for any form of substance abuse both times over the past two years!"

The attorney for the children's father tried to pounce on me again. "You still failed to follow through. You are unprofessional!!!" he screamed. But this time, the Judge put his finger up and pointed at the attorney. "Stop," the Judge said. "Stop and sit down." The attorney yelled, "Your Honor, I haven't finished my cross examination." But the Judge persisted. "Stop and sit down. Now!!" he said, raising his voice.

The attorney glared at me and then walked to his seat as the Judge had commanded him to do. The Judge then turned toward me and said, "Thanks for your testimony. You may step down." On my way down the stairs and back to the little waiting room, I glanced over at the ex husband and his attorney and was not surprised to see them glaring daggers at me. And as I passed my patient and her attorney, I heard her say "Way to go!"

About fifteen minutes after returning to the waiting room, I heard a commotion in the room next door to mine. There was loud talking and some yelling. "Maybe it's the attorneys trying to work out some kind of a deal," I thought to myself. Then, about five minutes after that, the attorney for my patient opened the door to my room, smiled and said: "Well, I guess you said something the Judge really liked. He found you to be a very credible, highly professional witness. He also found you to be very caring and empathic toward the children and their mother. As a result, he has decided to return partial custody to her as of today. Both kids will be spending time with her today." Unable to hide my delight, I jumped up and yelled "Thank you God!" And I had the pleasure of watching my patient hug her son and daughter as they got into her car and traveled home with her.

Do I think this all could have happened without the relaxing, calming impact of those deep, rapid style, Olympic breathing exercises? Most likely, not. But it was clear that for both my Anger – and the anxiety that followed – nothing worked more effectively than that last breathing exercise. In fact, one of my anger management participants told me that he would have to appear in court the following week… and wondered if these exercises could diminish both his anger and his anxiety. I advised him to give it a shot. He decided to do eight or ten of the in-out fast breathing exercises before entering the courtroom. The bottom line – the Judge said he noticed a distinct difference in the man. That he seemed much more agreeable and less combative. As a result, the Judge awarded him more visitation time with his young son. A great reward for using a highly effective breathing exercise!!

Breathing exercises definitely have a prominent place in controlling, diminishing and defusing the impact of Anger (and other powerful emotions as well.) But there are a few other effective techniques that I have recommended over the years. And based on the willingness of people to try them, these tools can prove extremely powerful.

You've heard the expression, "It's all in your mind." Well, let's start with one of the most basic mind experiences out there, and see if we can use it as a base for creating beliefs about our ability to control our Anger moving forward. The experience I'm talking about has been called "The Placebo Effect." You may have heard of it. The owner of a new Energy Pill company gathers ten people in a room and tells them that they will each be given a two week supply of his wham, bam, fantastic energy pills which he feels will have them soaring with energy before they know it. In two weeks, he says, they will all get together and talk about their experiences with the new energy pill.

What he doesn't tell the participants is that only half of them will get the actual energy pill. The other half – or five of the ten people – will be given sugar pills. No impact, do-nothing sugar pills.

So why, in God's name, do eight of the ten people come back in two weeks claiming to have more amazing energy and get-up-and-go than they've ever had before???!!! It's all in their heads, right? The fact is – and we've seen this many times – if we truly want to believe something, our minds will often be happy to accommodate us. And it's just this amazing tendency that can help us with visualizations that are perfect for defusing Anger just when it appears it will take over our lives.

One of the uniquely powerful visualizations that I share with my participants is almost too goofy to believe. Yet people can actually "feel" the anger leaving their bodies in a wild rush and powerful release when they do it. What is this magical visualization that is so highly effective, you ask? And how can you add it to your arsenal of anger control skills?

It goes something like this: You place both feet on the floor and sit upright in a straight back chair. Next, you hold your hands out in front of you, palms up as though you are about to grasp an imaginary bar bell. Now imagine that bar bell having some hefty weight on it. The most weight you have ever lifted in your life.

Now slowly lift that bar bell… higher and higher toward your chest. Feel the strain of the weight on your forearms and on your biceps. Now are you holding the bar bell close to your chest? I want you to hold it tight against yourself, and while you are doing so, I want you to imagine all the frustrations, all the things that piss you off, all the rage you have bottled up inside. Take all of that and load it onto the imaginary bar bell.

Now, when you're locked and loaded, slowly lower the bar bell. Slowly. Slowly. Now,

As the heavy bar bell moves lower and lower, extend your arms straight out in front of you and… OPEN YOUR FINGERS LIKE SPIDERMAN AND FLUSH OUT ALL THE ANGER, AND RAGE, AND FRUSTRATION INSIDE YOU!!! Feel the rush as you expel all those painful feelings from your body. Just like Spiderman discharges the white super webs that help him tie up the bad guys and swing from tall skyscrapers. Now relax in the knowledge that all the toxic junk is gone, and you are free to feel good again.

One of my anger management group participants stated that this mind exercise has served him and his young seven year old son so well, they do it every evening before they go to sleep. The man's son used to come home every day from school, complaining that other children were bullying him and ridiculing him. "I can't get to sleep thinking about those mean kids," he'd say to his Dad. But now after a few weeks of allowing their minds to believe that this exercise can sweep away all of their frustrations and anger from the day, they both get to sleep easily and effortlessly, believing that the toxic feelings have been released from their lives.

The mind is so funny in that way. Like a little puppy dog, it is often so willing to just happily follow us wherever we lead it. Tell it that a particular exercise like yoga or meditation calms us, and the mind believes it. Tell it that a particular act can change our day, or even our life, and the mind embraces it. So it is with the prior Spiderman Effect. And here's another exercise that illustrates the power of the mind's belief in that which helps it improve itself.

This next particular visualization is my favorite. It involves an experience that is common to many of us – having to deal with a nasty and unreasonable boss or supervisor at work. In this case, a young man in this early thirties named Joe had taken a new job as an assistant at a local savings and loan. Joe had worked in a similar capacity in the past in another city. He always thought of himself as a hard worker and was very happy to put his knowledge of finance and banking to use at this new job, especially since he had a young family to support.

Joe had only been at the job for a couple of weeks when he realized that his boss was not "the kind and gentle" type. In fact, as a former staff sergeant in the Armed Forces, his boss had kept that surly, "my way or the highway" edge that had apparently served him quite well during the Vietnam War. But now, in the little savings and loan office that Joe and his boss shared together, that hypercritical, demanding and insensitive attitude quickly put Joe on the defensive. In fact Joe was starting to resent his boss and the way he treated him, often in front of customers who came into the office to complete a transaction.

"God you're a dumb ass!" he'd bellow when Joe failed to get on the company website without asking for help. Or "Gee whiz! Why the Hell did I hire you?" he'd yell in front of a customer whom Joe was struggling to help complete a transaction. If Joe wasn't fast enough, sharp enough, confident enough, professional enough... he would constantly become the target of his boss's wrath. Day after day, Joe endured an avalanche of ridicule and mean spirited contempt. It got so bad that Joe sometimes envisioned himself getting up and sending a fist square into the face of his tormentor.

After several months of this treatment, it wasn't unusual for Joe to drive home, pull into the driveway, and just sit there shaking with rage at the end of a long, distasteful day. That's how much his boss's verbal abuse was hurting him. He knew that he wanted to just haul off and punch this jerk in the mouth. But if he did so, he would be immediately out of a job, something he simply couldn't afford to do. (Consequences!) With rent to pay, a car to pay off, food to buy, and a wife and young son to care for, he simply couldn't lose this job. That was a fact. But still the Anger he felt against his boss was bubbling and simmering with such intensity that it even affected the time he was not at work!

On this particular day, Joe had been particularly upset when his boss saw him struggling with a financial calculation on the computer, and scolded him. "Get up and let me fix that," he yelled. "Guess I've gotta do everything around here if I want it to be right." Recalling that miserable interaction in his mind, Joe got out of the car, and slammed the door as hard as he could. He started walking up the driveway toward his front door.

He walked up the steps to the house, angrily opened the door, and winced at the scene that met his eyes: his 7 year old's soccer ball and inline skates were lying right there in front of the door, blocking his path. "Dammit to hell," Joe screamed as he furiously kicked his son's toys out of the way. "What are you people trying to do," he bellowed. "Kill me and get my freakin' life insurance??"

Next he glanced over at the kitchen sink, and saw that a single coffee cup was sitting there in the basin. Still the sight of it infuriated Joe. "What are you doing," he screamed at his wife. "Sitting on your fat ass all day while I'm out killing myself???"

Now, Joe raised his hands to his head, and stormed into the living room. He sat down on the couch and suddenly a feeling of sadness and remorse washed over him. He realized that he was projecting all of the Anger and fury he felt toward his boss, onto his innocent wife and son! All of Joe's verbal aggression was spilling out on them because he was not able to deal with the Anger he was holding in against his boss. He knew in his heart that he was wrong to act this way toward the two people he loved most in the world… and he vowed to try to do something about it.

Next day was no different at the office. Same nasty, humiliating behavior by his boss. Same frustration building inside Joe, to the point where he wanted to explode. In fact, he did explode in a way, punching the wall in the restroom, leaving a small dent in the sheetrock. This was truly getting to be a problem. And Joe had no answers for dealing with it.

That evening Joe returned to his home. Pulling into the driveway, he grappled with the same rage and frustration that he felt every day after leaving the office. Once again seething with Anger, he sat remembering all the nasty things his boss had said to him that day. Once again, Joe jumped out of the car, and slamming the door, he began trudging up the driveway toward the house, carrying all of his rage with him.

But this time, Joe stopped dead in his tracks. He turned around and started walking quickly away from the house, down the driveway, and toward some trees that lined the edge of his front lawn. He looked left and right, making sure that none of his neighbors would see him doing what he was about to do. Suddenly he lunged forward and wrapped his arms around a healthy young maple tree that stood in front of him.

"Brother Tree," Joe pleaded, "I want you to take all the rage, all the fury, all the Anger I feel inside me against my boss... take it deep into your bark, into your trunk, and now, down, down through your roots, send it all deep into the ground around you. Free me from this burden!!! Thank you Brother Tree!!!

Having been freed of his burden of rage against his boss, Joe then turned up the driveway toward his house, made his way up the steps, and opened the front door. There, once again, his son's soccer ball and inline skates littered the front hallway. But this time Joe's reaction was different. Picking up the soccer ball, he yelled out "Where's my little All Star? Where's my beautiful wife?" He had found a mindful way of discharging the Anger that he held against his boss. And the result was a happier, more loving reality with his wife and son.

Visualizations like these, as weird as you may think they are, can actually "train the brain" to help discharge that powerful surge of angry energy before it is unleashed, helping us to avoid turning the object of our wrath into burnt toast. Such visualizations can also serve, if done regularly, to keep our individual level of rage at a lower ebb overall, insuring that we are less likely to bubble over into aggression when our worst triggers present themselves.

You may recall my discussion of meditation earlier, and how that simple technique of listening to your breath as it flows naturally through your nostrils is a powerful meditation in itself. Tough, hardened military veterans, who at first doubted its power, became convinced of its value. Now I'd like to invite you to explore other forms of meditation that can truly help.

One that really sticks out in my mind – and which I turn to each morning before I jump out of bed – is the "Ah" meditation. My wife Debbie had given me a CD featuring this specific meditation and told me that it was one of the most effective techniques used by internationally renowned meditation and spirituality guru Wayne Dyer.

I had heard of the "Om" meditation years earlier. Perhaps I connected it (probably incorrectly) to the Hari Krishna folks I saw chanting and dancing in the streets of the San Francisco Bay Area back in the days of Hippies, Street People and Hells Angels. I had never used that particular meditation but figured its origin was rooted in the culture of India and I really didn't explore it beyond that. This "Ah" meditation, my wife advised, was powerful in its own right... and was actually rooted in God, the Universe and our Higher Power. It was the sound of "Creation" she said, and offered those who chanted it and meditated on it, a unique pathway to peace, tranquility and personal control over our emotions – including anger.

Since my Anger continued to present daily challenges to me, I figured I'd give it a shot. With nothing to lose, I listened to the Wayne Dyer CD in which he encouraged those who meditated while saying "Ah" to simply imagine looking at a woodcut into which the word "Ah" was chiseled. I imagined that word chiseled into wood, and proceeded to chant the word "Ah."

The time I decided to do so was during those first moments right after awakening in the morning. I closed my eyes, imagined the word "Ah" etched into that woodcut in my mind, and lightly vocalized "Ah" just as I used to do at the dentist's office. "Ah," "Ah," "Ah." Over and over, I would express the word. A unique calmness would suddenly wash over me. After doing twenty or so incantations, I would end the meditation by saying my last "Ah," followed by "God" vocalized in the same manner.

The crazy thing about this – and something I share with all of my anger management participants – is that, not only does the word "God" rhyme with "Ah" (along with "Amen" and "Alleluia") but the sound "Ah" is in the name for God in virtually every religion. Jehovah, Allah, Yahweh, Buddha, Ra, Messiah, Ja... the list goes on and on!

Now it's not like the Muslims called the Buddhists, who called the Jews, who called the Christians, and so on, and they all decided to put the "Ah" sound in their own individual name for God. So how did this strange little synchronicity occur? Who knows. All I know is that every day I do that meditation, for at least five minutes in the morning, my day goes better. I am calmer. Fewer things upset me. My triggers don't seem to find me on those days. And even if they do, I don't let them unleash my anger in the form of the verbal or physical aggression that leads to consequences. It's that simple. And I recommend it. Definitely worth a try.

CHAPTER 6
TURNING THE ANGER KALEIDOSCOPE

Ever had a kaleidoscope when you were a kid? They're really a lot of fun and quite magical. You get to look through one end while turning the other end to reveal multiple, quite beautiful configurations of color glass. Holding it up toward the sun or other light makes the experience even more interesting and enjoyable.

But say you picked one up for the first time. And you were unaware that you could turn one end, while gazing through the other. And say the image that you saw when you picked the kaleidoscope up was one of dreary, rainy day colors like dark gray, and dark blue. You might say to yourself, "What a stupid, dull instrument this is!" and throw it away. But that would be so sad because in reality, that one kaleidoscope is capable of presenting hundreds, even thousands, of unique images... with colors ranging from bright oranges and yellows to light blues, shimmering greens, and vibrant violets. You would simply have to turn the kaleidoscope to see something amazingly different from the stagnant, lifeless image you originally perceived and were convinced was all there was to see.

Life is a lot like that. When an event occurs, we have a tendency to see one – and only one – side of the situation. We fail to "turn the kaleidoscope" and challenge our beliefs and perception about what we have just witnessed. We don't ask ourselves if some other variable might be at play here. As a result we may jump to conclusions. And the consequence of that action might be that we become judge, jury and executioner, stuck in our one belief, and if the belief is making us angry, then we can start going up the Mindfulness Pyramid – maybe even all the way up to "Enraged." And we may actually be wrong!

Famous psychotherapist Albert Ellis came up with what he called the ABCD Model in which, like my story of the kaleidoscope, he recommended that people challenge their initial belief regarding a distressing, anger producing person or event. In his model, A stands for Activating Event. B for Belief. C stands for Consequences. And D stands for "Dispute." How, Ellis asks, can we dispute our initial belief and possibly come up with a different belief or impression that will leave us less angry, less frustrated and less likely to act in a way that leads to negative consequences?

Turning the kaleidoscope holds the key. This story appeared in the Federal booklet I referenced in Chapter 3. Imagine somebody cuts you off while you're driving on a heavily traveled road. Without any signal or notice. But they don't angrily flash you the "FU" sign. They just go flying past at top speed. Now that's what Ellis would call the Activating Event. But it's not the event itself that pisses you off. Rather it's your BELIEF about the event that really gets you going up the anger scale. "That person was a real nasty SOB!" you might rage. "How dare he do that to me! I could have been killed!" C stands for the Consequences of believing what you do. And that could mean watching your blood pressure soar through the roof, cursing and swearing, and possibly even following the other driver, and maybe even getting into an altercation with him or her. D stands for Dispute. Dispute offers you a simple chance to contest the belief that has you in such a tizzy, ready to unleash all of your anger and fury.

Again, it's like turning the kaleidoscope. Let's try it here. What other "belief" might you substitute for the belief that has you all pissed off... heading toward being enraged? Is it possible for example that the person who cut you off did so for a reason other than selfish recklessness? What if the driver had just received word from his brother, for example, that his mother had just suffered a massive stroke. And the driver was speeding to get to the hospital before she passed away. Or maybe, just maybe, the driver was speeding because his pregnant wife was in the back seat, about to give birth to their first child at any minute, and he was trying to get her to the hospital before the baby arrived. That's why he cut you off. Or maybe the driver was a volunteer fireman who was trying to get to the scene of a fire to save several young children who were trapped in the upstairs of a burning home? He didn't have his blue flashing light with him, so you didn't know he was a fireman. Any of these situations would likely have knocked your level of Anger down from the Enraged zone to possibly just feeling ticked off or peeved.

If you simply said to yourself (as you disputed your original belief) that you were going to give the driver the benefit of the doubt, that it might have been an emergency, that you weren't hurt, that the car was not damaged and that you would likely get to work on time – now your anger level is so much lower. And with this belief you are likely to avoid the consequences that you might have suffered had you continued to believe that the driver was just "a careless SOB." Essentially, you turned the kaleidoscope, tried to change your belief about what happened, and as a result, you were a lot less angry.

I like to use this model in my Anger Management Groups to dissect a situation in my own life that used to have me in the "Enraged zone" every time I faced it. I shudder to think of how pig-headed and blind I was — not just for a short time... but for YEARS!!! That situation presented itself many times in my life. And every time I acted exactly the same way: angry, frustrated, bewildered, judgmental and enraged. I was convinced that I was right and that the object of my wrath – my own Doctor – was wrong. And my belief persisted for over six long years until I finally turned the kaleidoscope and saw that my belief about him was absolutely warped, distorted, and dead wrong.

Fact is, I was convinced that – because I would always have to languish impatiently at least forty five minutes to an hour in his waiting room before being seen – my doctor was a goof-off, a numbskull, an inefficient, careless boob who couldn't care less that I had to leave my staff meeting at work early, just to sit for an hour waiting and waiting and waiting in his damned waiting room! There I'd be, sitting with my stupid 3 month old copy of Ladies Home Journal, or Better Homes & Gardens, hoping that I'd be freed from my waiting room prison. But no. The torture always continued endlessly.

And there was no shortage of rageful, negative imagery simmering in my brain. To me, he was the biggest piece of crap on the planet. I imagined him sitting in his office with his feet up on his desk. Munching on a deli sandwich... or maybe playing video games... while I and other patients languished in his waiting room. I imagined him also looking on with great interest as some elderly patient showed him photo after photo after photo of her grandchildren during the family's most recent holiday cruise to the islands. Or maybe the good doctor was gleefully chasing his pretty female assistant around the nurse's station. I even imagined him peeking through the curtain at the doorway between the waiting room and his back offices, eyeing me in my growing distress, and laughing uncontrollably over the torment he was causing me!

Yes, I had clearly reached the Enraged zone and that put me precipitously close to flipping out and creating a rageful disturbance that could end in nothing short of serious consequences for me! I even recall going up to the poor receptionist once with my copy of Ladies Home Journal in hand…seething over having to wait nearly an hour once again. Being told to come at 3 pm and having the clock right above me striking 4 pm. Oh, I wanted to strike someone all right! I walked right up to that poor receptionist and growled "Does he even know that I'm out here?? I've been waiting nearly an hour now and there is no sign the Doctor is even close to calling me in for my appointment!!" And at that, I'd hurl my copy of Ladies Home Journal against the nearest chair, as if to emphatically underscore my point. Oh yes, I was judge, jury and executioner. I knew what that miserable doctor was up to. I even dared to say these words to the now fear-stricken receptionist: "Maybe I ought to just leave. Leave right now. How'd the good doctor like that?" But in the pit of my stomach, I knew he couldn't care less. And I, in order to address the malady I had come for in the first place, would just be cutting my nose off to spite my face. The next day, I'd be calling the nurse begging for a second chance to come in and be seen.

Well, in any case, I was absolutely, positively certain beyond a shadow of a doubt that this doctor was a total, uncaring screw-up. But I was about to get a lesson using the ABCD model that would shake me to the very core of my being and show me how nasty and twisted and detrimental it can be when we enable ourselves to become judge, jury and executioner. Only to find out we are dead wrong!!!

What woke me up? Well the story goes back to fall of 2016. I was working as a therapist at a nearby clinic and one lovely afternoon in October I happened to notice something that ticked me off as I pulled out of my driveway. There, in front of me, wrapped around one of the pine trees that bordered our property, was a leafy vine that looked as though it might choke the tree, and maybe even kill it. Well, I was having none of that. I leapt out of the car, raced up to the tree, yanked at that leafy vine, and pulled it from its roots. And I didn't give a damn if those leaves touched my arms or hands as I yanked at the vine. Even if it was poison ivy, poison zumac, or poison oak Why? Because in all of my 67 years of life, I had never suffered from any of them. I was certain of that. Positive. Sure as the day is long. Until the next day, when I discovered little raised bumps all over my left forearm.

Imagine my surprise as I awoke that morning, and felt the urge to scratch those little raised bumps. So yielding to the urge, I scratched... and scratched... and scratched. Whatever belief I had nurtured all these years that I was in no way vulnerable to poison ivy – or any of the poison leafy plants for that matter – instantly went out the window. I was itching. And itching not just on my left forearm, but now on my chest... on my upper left thigh... and even on my neck. I was in big trouble!! Desperately I searched the medicine cabinet hoping against hope that I would find something, anything that would soothe the maddening itch. After 20 minutes of fruitless hunting through the medicine cabinet, the bathroom closet and virtually every other cabinet and closet in the house... I fell onto the coach, exhausted and defeated. I would have to venture out to the nearest pharmacy and see what they might have in stock to address my growing pain and frustration.

So that Sunday afternoon I found myself in our local drug store, rifling through the anti itch, anti poison ivy products on the shelves. Since I had never had poison ivy before, I had no clue as to what would work or what I should buy. I finally settled on a bottle of calamine lotion. A friend had told me that this had worked for him, and would likely help me as well. I grabbed the small pinkish bottle and headed for the counter. I began to feel some hope that maybe I could get this annoying little affliction under control.

I was sadly mistaken. After slathering gobs of the pink liquid on my arms in the car, I arrived home in my driveway ready to scream in anguish, with an even greater urge to dig my finger nails deep into both forearms and scratch, scratch, scratch. I ran into the house and went on line to see if anything else might be available to me. I found a product that was exorbitantly priced, but promised with its tiny anti itch granules to "stop poison ivy in its tracks!" But only if it's applied early in the infection. Was it still early enough in my infection? Could this product possibly work? At that point I would pay almost anything for some hint of relief. I looked at my watch. It was almost six on a Sunday evening. No way my local drug store was still open. I bit my lip, slathered more calamine lotion on my arms, and vowed to be at the drug store as soon as it opened the next day.

After a restless night of itching, scratching, spreading, poison ivy hell, I was nearly beside myself. Even getting dressed for work was a total nightmare. As my dear spouse helped my pull my sleeves over my infected arms and chest, I hoped against hope that the drug store really had something that could help me. First on line as the door was open, I raced to the anti itch aisle. There, before me, was the product I had read about online the night before. With packaging that declared it the "cure" for poison ivy, I headed for the check out counter, finally believing that I was about to get the relief I craved. I left the drug store and headed to my office with a new feeling of hope.

Not so fast. As I fumbled with the bottle in the rest room at my office and finally yanked the top off, I read in tiny print on the back of the box the following words: "Massage tiny granules into the affected area within 10 to 12 hours of infection." Had it been 10 to 12 hours since I wrestled with the poison ivy vine that was wrapped around the tree? Or was it more like 16 or 20 hours. Oh crap! It was the latter for sure. Now, I found myself applying the granules anyway… and hoping against hope that I was in time to thwart the advance of this insidious infection.

The entire drive to the office, I tried to talk myself into believing that the itching was subsiding. But that was 30 minutes ago. Now I sat at my desk and stared into space. I had group therapy in ten minutes and here I was ready to jump out of my skin, as new patches of infection began to make themselves known to me under my dress shirt. I was beside myself. This new product wasn't working after all!

Needless to say this was the day from hell. Scratching and scratching between writing reports and facilitating group and individual therapy, I was ready to cry. Nothing I had done had helped. My last resort – going to another pharmacy and begging the pharmacist to tell me that he had SOMETHING to soothe my agonizing, frustratingly maddening affliction.

As 5 o'clock rolled round, I grabbed my car keys and raced to the pharmacy a few blocks from the office. This was one of those mega drug stores. If anyone had something, it was them.

I waited impatiently until I was able to finally get the pharmacist's attention. "Please," I begged, "What do you have for an infection like this???" I rolled up my sleeves to reveal two forearms that were blood red with pus and deep, nasty scratches. I will never forget the pharmacist's response.

"We don't really have anything for a poison ivy infection that advanced," he replied, surveying the ravaged arms over his horn rimmed glasses. He frowned as if to say, "You've got it really, really bad."

The words he said next shattered my day… and left me speechless. "I think you are going to have to go to your doctor and get a prescription for something strong," he mused. "That's my recommendation."

I nearly fell through the floor. The LAST THING I WANTED TO DO was go to my doctor!!! I hated my doctor. He was the jerk who made me wait over an hour every time I came for an appointment. The guy I imagined sitting with his feet up on the desk… or chasing his nurse around the nurse's station… or fawning over some grandma's vacation photos of her grandkids. While I and twenty other people languished in his waiting room. Hoping against hope that he'd finally ask us to come back to his office.

But somewhere deep in my soul, I knew the pharmacist was right. I had to suck it up... overcome my feelings of disdain and hatred for my doctor... and call his office. I needed relief that bad!!!

I gulped hard, thanked the pharmacist for his help, and headed for my car in the parking lot. As I opened the car door, I realized that I could wait no longer. I simply had to call and see if I could finally get some relief even if it meant going back to that "knuckled head" doctor of mine.

As I dialed the number, a million thoughts raced through my mind. Would I have to leave work early again? Would he even see me right away? Could I hold my temper if I had to deal with that horrible waiting room again? The "rrrinnngg" of his office phone sounded in my ear. I held my breath... and then the nurse picked up.

"Hello, this is Joanne at Dr. Smith's office. How can I help you?" I blurted out my name and predicament in a torrent of mixed frustration, pain and despair. "Joanne," I begged, "is there any way the doctor can help me out. I have a raging case of poison ivy and I just don't know what to do. I have literally tried every over the counter medicine there is. Could he possibly help me today or tomorrow?"

There was a pause on the other end of the line. "David, I really don't think he can take time out today. The lobby is filled with patients waiting to see him. I don't even know if he can see you tomorrow. Give me a chance to speak with him. I'll call you back in 10 minutes."

That next ten minutes was like an eternity. Finally my phone rang, and much to my surprise, I heard the following: "Well David, I don't know I got him to do it, but he dropped everything, and went on the computer to check what meds you're currently on. He saw that none of your meds would conflict what he wants to prescribe for you. Then he sat down, wrote the prescription for you, and called the script into the Wal-Mart Pharmacy. You can go and pick up the medicine this afternoon."

"Oh my God, that's awesome!" I yelled over the phone. "Please tell the doctor I am sooo grateful! Please thank him for me Joanne!" When I hung up, I just sat for a moment. The grin on my face was ear to ear. I was FINALLY going to get some relief from this horrible, horrible poison ivy. I couldn't wait to pick up the meds and put myself out of my misery. I can happily report that within 12 hours of taking the first tablet, my poison ivy had virtually disappeared!

Perhaps more importantly, I was absolutely so grateful that my doctor had taken the time to help me that I no longer had that nasty hatred toward him that had burned inside me for so long. In fact it was time for me to turn the kaleidoscope and rethink that Belief in the ABCD Model that had made me judge, jury and executioner as far as my doctor was concerned. Maybe – just maybe – I was wrong. Turning that kaleidoscope helped me see things in a whole new light! In fact it only took another visit to my doctor about a month later to confirm that my Belief about my doctor – which I held for so long – was finally about to be Disputed!

Yes, as I returned to see him for a pulled muscle in my leg, I began to realize how wrong I had truly been. As I recalled the way he dropped everything to write and call in my prescription to end that raging poison ivy once and for all, I began to think: If my doctor did that for me, he probably showed the same caring behavior toward other patients who called in with emergencies. Like the Mom who calls because her two year old son has opened a kitchen cabinet and ingested a bottle of furniture wax. Or the carpenter who calls in because in the middle of putting up sheet rock, he suddenly feels the entire left side of his face go numb. Or the elderly lady who calls in to say that she's having intense heart pains… and can't get her cardiologist on the phone.

The bottom line is that I had judged my Doctor for over five years as being a self-centered, lazy, disorganized loser. By turning the kaleidoscope, albeit because of my own health emergency that left me crazed and helpless, I was finally able to get a different view of him. A view that said: "This guy is such a caring, amazing Doctor that he's actually <u>fielding phone calls</u> in the midst of a non-stop busy day in an office packed with sick patients!" If anything, it's just the opposite of what I thought. This man is so dedicated to his patients that nothing will get between him and the care of his patients – whether they are standing in his office, or miles away.

I later learned that the medical group that managed my Doctor's practice was actually upset with him. The reason? He took "way too much time with his patients!" In fact, they apparently wanted him to spend less than seven minutes with each patient. He was giving each patient more like twelve or thirteen minutes. So his caring nature actually clashed with the business model of his medical group whose focus was on the bottom line.

Thus the ABCD model taught me an amazingly powerful lesson. A lesson that compels me to challenge my thinking every time I get pissed off at someone who fails to do what I expect, or something that fails to go my way. Using the ABCD model hit a nerve with many of my anger management participants. One man in particular spelled out how he himself was judge jury and executioner with a situation that had him viewing his wife as a lazy, good-for-nothing coach potato… when in reality he was dead wrong.

In his case, it started one evening when he returned home from a long day at work in the city. He had worked hard at his job, endured the long train ride home, and was now looking forward to spending a quiet, restful evening at home with his family. But that scenario was not what he experienced when he entered the door that particular evening.

In fact, his two sons, 8 and 9 years old, where wrestling on the living room carpet, while loud music blared from the stereo system. The stove was cold. A pile of dishes sat in the sink and dinner appeared to be a far off dream. So that dire scene he witnessed right there was A, the Activating Event. But it was B, his Belief about the situation, that really got his blood boiling. His Belief was that since he worked so hard in the city, chained to his desk all day, the least he could expect was that his wife of ten years would have a hot meal on the table... the house would be neat... and their two sons would be quietly studying in their rooms. This Belief immediately led to some nasty Consequences. The "C" in the ABCD Model.

His blood pressure soared as he reprimanded his sons for their loud, uncontrolled behavior. He then angrily strode past the dirty dishes, past the messy living room, and headed upstairs to here his wife was neatly tucked in bed, watching the Oprah Show on TV. Since his Belief was that his wife was ignoring her duties – and actually just a lazy so-and-so – the Consequences reflected that belief. He got red in the face. He angrily snarled at his wife about shirking her parental responsibilities. He lambasted her for not cooking the evening meal. Blasted her for not keeping their sons under control. And called her everything from lazy and loser, to a failure as a wife and mother. He was so certain of this... that he allowed himself to reach the "Enraged" zone... pummeling her with criticisms. He punctuated it all by hurling a pillow at the TV set, and storming out of the room.

That evening he ate alone, making himself a sandwich. He was angry and he felt he definitely had a right to be angry. After all his wife was "doing nothing for their family" while he was out busting his ass. But you know what? He failed to apply the ABCD Model to the situation. His failure to do so made him look like the real loser when the truth came out.

You see, several days after his angry tirade in which he berated his wife for all of her failures, he received a call from his wife's physician. He couldn't believe what his ears were hearing. "Your wife has the first signs of Multiple Sclerosis," the physician stated. As the man listened to his wife's doctor describe her developing illness, his eyes filled with tears. "You see," the doctor continued, "your wife has been unable to stand recently without feeling very dizzy. You may not know this, but she has already fallen twice in your home. A feeling of dizziness and vertigo are initial symptoms of this disease. Also she is losing her ability to see objects clearly. She has been lying in bed more and more because she is fearful of falling. She told me she has been hiding all of this from you, because she had hoped the symptoms would go away. She said she feels that she has disappointed you terribly. I am calling to let you know that this disease is serious and we have to begin treatments right away."

When the man hung up the phone, he was devastated. He had judged his wife as a lazy, uncooperative person and it turned out he was dead wrong. You can imagine his feelings of sadness and remorse upon hearing the news from her doctor. And think about all the angry evenings, heart breaking conversations, and wasted opportunities to show love and family unity. Once again, a simple commitment to the ABCD model and a firm decision to dispute our initial thoughts by using the kaleidoscope, and looking at every situation that angers us from a different perspective, can make all the difference.

Here's another example of how we tend to jump to conclusions, take things personally, and boil out of control... leaving ourselves so dead certain that all we want to do is let the object of our wrath have it right between the eyes!

In this particular case, a young father comes home early from his job in the city with one thing in mind: He wants to surprise his beloved wife at the end of a long work day by cooking an amazing meal that he, his wife and their children will enjoy and remember for years to come. So he dons his apron, sets the dining room table, puts candles and the best silverware out, and then proceeds to prepare his wife's dream dinner, replete with roast beef, mashed potatoes and gravy, asparagus, and cranberry sauce. So out come the pots and pans and mixing bowls. His labor of love knows no bounds as he determines to treat his young wife to the best home cooked dinner she's every had. And of course it will mean that – at least for once – she will not have to scurry around once she's home getting a meal cooked for the family. Thanks to her loving husband, it will all be done and she will sit down to the feast without having had to lift a finger.

Throughout his cooking experience, the husband of course makes a mess but cleans it up, and even engages the children in the process by getting them to pick the nicest table cloth and set the good china out. The husband has a self-satisfied smile on his face throughout the process, imagining just how delighted his wife will be when she comes in the front door and witnesses the feast he has lovingly prepared for her!

But while all these lovely preparations are being made, the husband doesn't have a clue about the kind of horrible day that his young wife, a 2nd grade teacher in the city school district, is experiencing. Almost from the moment she left this morning, this nasty day has shaped up as one of her toughest experiences ever. She starts out by having to endure the rude, bitchy behavior of the lady who sold her a cup of coffee and a bagel at the local donut shop. And it all goes downhill from there.

Once his wife arrives at her school, she finds her 2nd grade classroom in complete disarray. Several of the young boys are engaged in a fistfight. Calling each other names. Throwing erasers at each other. When she steps in to stop the kids from beating each other up, one of the little punks turns around and bites her firmly on her right wrist. Screaming in pain, she ends up yelling at the disruptive students to sit down. Meanwhile she finds that she can't stop the blood that's oozing from the bite marks on her arm.

Rushing down the hall to the school nurse's office, she barges in, weeping loudly over both her injury as well as over her inability to get her classroom under control. The nurse bandages the bite wound and even calls the local hospital as she surveys the damage, and wonders if the injury might just require stitches to close it properly.

After nearly a half hour, she summons the courage and energy to return to her classroom. By this time, the substitute teacher is nearly pulling her hair out, desperately trying to get the kids to focus on the lessons at hand. She greets the man's wife by grabbing her books and purse, and marching angrily out the door.

Meanwhile the deepest cut of all is about to come when the Principal stops by and says, "Mrs Green, may I see you in my office at 3 o'clock?" She hangs her head, sadly realizing that this can't be a good thing. When she arrives there later, the Principal reprimands her for her inability to control her class, criticizes her teaching style and then says something that sends a chill through her: "I've been receiving many complaints from the parents about you. It's gotten so bad, I have no choice but to think about letting you go. Let's give you a month to see if you can get your act together… otherwise I'll have no choice but to relieve you of your duties here at PS 191. I'm sorry."

On the long drive home, the man's wife is crying uncontrollably, matching the raindrops that are pounding relentlessly against her windshield. The door to door trip is bad enough at 20 something miles on highly congested area highways. But now she stares out of her windshield at a sea of red lights in front of her. The radio blares the news. A three car pile up several miles ahead of her has caused all traffic to stop. She's in a virtual parking lot for the next 45 minutes.

After limping home in her little car, she is emotionally spent, recognizing that she has truly just experienced the day from hell. She is tired, humiliated, fearful and sick to her stomach. And now she is about to open the door to her home at the end of this horrific day.

Her husband yells "Surprise!" as he gestures toward the dinner simmering on the stove and the beautifully set dining room table. But she meets his enthusiasm with nothing but a cold, scornful gaze, and a deadening silence.

The husband can't believe his eyes! "What the hell!! Are you F-ing kidding me???!!!" he screams in rageful disbelief. "I have cooked this amazing dinner... made the dessert... set the table... all as a surprise for you – And THIS is what I get???!!!" His fury at her behavior now knows no bounds. He yanks the beautiful roast out of the oven and dumps it in the trash. He pulls the mashed potatoes and asparagus off the stove top and dumps them as well... all the time screaming and cursing at the top of his lungs. His wife starts screaming now at the top of her lungs... releasing all the misery and anger that she's been bottling up from her hellish day at work. The kids now start screaming too. The dinner is a complete disaster. The kids race up to bed hungry. The husband throws his coat on and heads for the door. His wife collapses on the living room couch, weeping her eyes out. The night is ruined.

Now, imagine for just a moment, that the husband had used the ABCD model and turned the kaleidoscope ever so slightly in regard to his wife's behavior. If he had challenged his Belief regarding her behavior, the night might have had a totally different ending. Let's check out the thought process that got him to the point of utter rage and fury: First, the Activating Event is clearly his wife's miserable, unhappy facial expression and defeated body language when she walks in the door. In his mind, anything short of a jubilant, happily surprised expression from his wife was unacceptable. Taking her facial expression personally – and not considering any other cause for her sour disposition – of course he was going to be angry. His Belief was clearly that she DID NOT APPRECIATE all the hard work he had put into the dinner. After all, he had left his job early, rushed home before her, put on his apron, studied the recipe for her favorite meal, set the table, slaved over a hot stove, made the dessert – AND THIS IS WHAT HE GETS for all the love and caring affection he put into this act of genuine kindness???!!! The Consequences that followed were easy to predict. Believing that she was nothing but "a callous, disrespectful and uncaring ingrate," he vigorously tore apart all the good work he had done. All in a vicious, punitive rage.

BUT WHAT IF HE HAD DISPUTED HIS BELIEF??? If, for only a second, he had turned the kaleidoscope, and looked at the situation through a different lens, he might have seen his wife's painful expression from a completely different perspective and the night might have been saved. All it would have taken was a decision on his part to challenge the Belief that caused him to race up to the top of the Anger Pyramid.

Think about it. He knew that she had a long, difficult commute to her job. Traffic jams. Accidents. Delays. It was almost a daily occurrence. He also knew from the past that sometimes those 2nd grade brats had made his wife's life miserable. Many days she had complained about not having the support of the principal in helping her to keep this unruly bunch of very young children under control. It was all on her, and many days she found herself on the verge of tears because of their terrible behavior. He also knew that his wife had been treated rudely by the Principal and other teachers in the past.

Now factor in the things he DIDN'T KNOW about her day from hell – the bloody bite on her arm, the students' fist fight that led up to the biting incident, the complaints against her by the parents, the Principal's decision to put her on probation – and all of a sudden, maybe, just maybe, the husband's Belief that his wife's scowling, disgruntled face was all about him was actually ALL WRONG!

Let's rewind the tape and pretend that the husband did use the ABCD Model to help him through this situation. This time, as she comes in the door, and he notices her unhappy face, he might feel pissed at first but now he challenges his perception. "Wait a minute," he thinks. "Her facial expression might not be related to me at all, but to something completely different. Maybe she had a hellish day at school. Is that what's eating her? Did she possibly get in an accident? Were the teachers rude to her? Maybe I'm taking this personally and the poor thing has been through something horrible. And that's the reason for that look on her face."

His next thought – "Maybe I can help her." So he changes his approach. "Oh honey, did you have an awful day at that god-forsaken school? You look like you've got the weight of the world on your shoulders love. Come on in and sit down in the living room. Take a load off your feet… and let me get your slippers and a glass of wine. It's all going to be all right."

His wife can't believe her ears. She collapses in the living room, bursting into grateful tears that finally – finally – someone is listening to her. Someone cares enough to find out what actually happened to her. The husband embraces his wife and tells her it's all going to be all right. "They don't deserve you at that school," he says supportively. "And that terrible commute. Maybe it's time to find a school closer to home, where you don't have to go through this crap every day. Well, you just take a few minutes to relax and decompress. When you're ready hon, come and join me and the kids for your favorite dinner. I prepared it with love. Just for you!"

Wow! What a difference a turn of the kaleidoscope makes. By now, the husband can clearly see that his original Belief about his wife's behavior was completely wrong. By Disputing his initial thoughts, he gave himself a chance not just to find the REAL reason for his wife's miserable facial expression and body language… but to SAVE the entire evening and enjoy all the love he had put into the special dinner preparations he had created for his beloved wife.

Now, of course just because he turned the kaleidoscope didn't guarantee that his wife's facial expression was a reflection of her horrible day at school – and not directed at her husband.

But this is a perfect example of how often in life many of us jump to conclusions about what's going on. How we become Judge, Jury and Executioner toward virtually everyone and everything that crosses our path and may strike us as being negative or unfriendly toward us. Just as I failed to use the ABCD Model when viewing my Doctor's inability to see me on a timely basis…

and judged and condemned him as a lazy, inefficient and careless screw-up… (when he was really fielding emergency phone calls while trying to treat all the patients in his office) we have a tendency to PERSONALIZE our experiences. And we fail to realize that, more often than not, a quick turn of the kaleidoscope can reveal underlying reasons and issues that we had never imagined on our wildest dreams. And THAT my friend is the value of the ABCD Model. Thank you Albert Ellis!!!

CHAPTER 7

BE ASSERTIVE, NOT AGGRESSIVE... TO GET WHAT YOU WANT

In this all important chapter we are going to explore the difference between being Assertive... and deciding to choose other forms of behavior when we are upset, frustrated or angry about something in our lives.

It still astounds me that many, many people feel that being Aggressive – either physically or verbally – can get positive results for us. We may get someone's attention. We may strike fear into the heart of someone. We may terrorize them into doing what we want them to do. But when it comes right down to it, Aggressive behavior of any kind usually leads to the kind of consequences that we may regret for the rest of our lives. Like going to jail. Losing a job. Destroying a relationship. All those good things.

When I reach this part of my program with a participant, or group of participants, I can often detect their confusion and frustration over the basic terms that we are using. So I begin by asking them to draw a simple diagram that enables them to better understand the differences between various behaviors.

We start by drawing a straight horizontal line from one side of the page to the other. In the very middle, I ask them then to draw a short vertical line through the horizontal line. And above that line I ask them to write the word "Assertiveness." Below the line I ask them to write the following definition: "Speaking up for ourselves in a firm, but respectful manner." Then, at the extreme right side of the horizontal line, I ask them to write the words "Physical and Verbal Aggression." On the extreme left side of the horizontal line, I ask them to write the words "Passive Aggressive Behavior."

With that simple set up, we are now able to begin our discussion of Assertiveness and why, among all other actions, it is the behavior of choice in resolving issues that have us soaring up the Anger Pyramid toward the enraged zone. By being assertive we actually have a good chance of resolving a situation in a way that not only keeps us out of jail… but actually leads to a positive outcome for us.

Our discussion of Assertiveness begins with a story about my imaginary experience as a Carpenter for a major company that builds houses in a suburb of the eastern United States. Are you kidding? Me a real Carpenter? I'm lucky if I don't smack my thumb with the hammer when I'm putting a frame on the wall. Anyway, in this particular example, I am nonetheless, a Carpenter who has worked for ten years for this company, framing houses, barns, and sheds… while also building foundations, putting up sheetrock, painting walls, etc. You get the idea.

One day, while I'm working on framing a new house, my boss – the Contractor with whom I've worked amicably and productively over the past ten years – walks up the hill from his office to pay me a visit. I stop my hammering, wipe my sweaty brow and step forward to hear what he has to say.

"Dave I've got some bad news," is the first thing out of his mouth. Then it goes downhill from there. "As you know," he says, "It's been a bad year for the company. With the economic downturn, we simply haven't been selling as many houses as before. As a result, I'm sorry to say that I have to cut you $5 bucks an hour starting today. And that overtime work on the weekends? I can't do that anymore either. Sorry Dave. That's just the way it is."

For a moment I stared at him blankly, not sure what to say. It is precisely at this moment that we choose our path: either to be assertive, aggressive or passive aggressive in attempting to deal with this painful moment. Let's choose to be assertive here just to give you a clear idea of what the preferred way of dealing with something that angers us really looks like.

I take a deep breath, summon my thoughts and then speak up for myself in a firm but respectful manner: "Wow, boss. A $5 buck an hour cut? I can't take a $5 buck hour cut. I mean I got my truck to pay off, my rent to pay, and my family to support. I just can't take a financial hit like that. And though I'd hate to leave this company after ten years… I got to believe that *somebody* in the Hudson Valley will pay me what I'm worth."

I catch my breath and then I proceed respectfully. "You know boss, you and I have been a great team over the past ten years. And I like working here. And I also know that the last thing you want to do is to have to hire some new guy to come in and take my place, and learn all the blueprints that I have down cold. That would be a task I'm sure you'd like to avoid."

"But you know, I don't really want to leave. How about we put our heads together and see if there isn't some other way you can trim costs without having to cut me $5 bucks an hour."

At this point I can see that my boss is listening intently. Heck, I've been firm but respectful… so why shouldn't he listen to me? And this assertive approach is my best chance of resolving this problem that has me feeling frustrated, angry and uncertain about my future.

I continue, "I have a few ideas on how we might cut costs if you don't mind. For example, one of the things I admire you for is how you always go top of the line when you purchase wood. That wood you buy from that supplier up on Millbrook is the best out there.

But the fact is that you have me using that top notch wood not just for framing the houses, but for framing our barns and garages and sheds too. Now, if you were to consider getting the wood for those out buildings from say, Home Depot or Lowes, you could probably save 40%. I could continue to frame the houses with the expensive wood from the guy in Millbrook. And for the sheds and out buildings I could use the less pricey wood. That would save you a bundle right there." My boss nodded his head, and I could see that he acknowledged I had a point.

I was on an assertive roll here, being respectful of him but truly speaking my mind. "I was also thinking about the paint we use. You're paying over $40 bucks a can for that top of the line Benjamin Moore paint. And I admire you for that. But you know, you've got me using that $40 paint not just on the living rooms, dining rooms and bedrooms in the house… but I'm using that same paint to cover the insides of the garages and the unfinished basement areas, and we don't even know if the buyers are going to use the basement area for living space."

"Now if we went to Lowe's we could get their $12 a can paint and use that to cover those areas that aren't prime living space. And you could save a ton of money right there as well."

Now, I can see that my boss is really thinking about what I've just said and he's really considering it. Slowly, he opens his mouth and says the words that are music to my ears: "Now Dave I can't promise anything. But you do make some very good sense. And I know for sure that I don't want to lose you… and have to train some new guy to do what you've been doing effectively over the past ten years. How about you come by my office after work today. We'll sit down over a cup of coffee and see if we can't work something out. Because I value your work, and you've been a big part of our success here."

Bingo! That's what Assertiveness can get for you. Was I angry and pissed off when I first heard he wants to cut my salary and my overtime?? Absolutely! But I remained calm, and I stood up for myself in a firm but respectful manner. It was that approach – never allowing myself to behave in a verbally or physically aggressive way – that opened things up to the point where I just might get what I was hoping for: the ability to retain my job, at a place where I like working, while NOT suffering a cut in pay which would have truly impacted myself and my family in a negative way.

You can imagine what the Physically or Verbally Aggressive version of the above behavior might be. So let's go through the aforementioned scenario once again: My boss walks up the hill. Looks me in the eye and says "Sorry Dave, but we're just not selling as many houses this year as we have in the past. So I'm going to have to cut you five bucks an hour starting right away. And that weekend overtime work – I just can't do it anymore. Sorry."

Well, in the following scenario I don't even think about remaining calm and respectful. I'm pissed and the consequences of my actions are the furthest thing from my mind! "Are you fu..ing kidding me?" I scream. "Ten years of coming in here and working in every kind of weather – freezing rain, snow, ice, you name it – just to help you make your deadlines! And THIS is the bullsh.. I get!!!!!"

My boss winces at my verbal tirade and says once again how sorry he is. He turns around and starts walking down the hill, and back to his office. And I am fit to be tied. I continue my tirade to myself, with no one in particular in earshot. "That SOB," I scream. "I thought he was coming up the hill to give me a raise. And he tells me he's gonna cut me five bucks an hour???!!! He's gotta be out of his frickin' mind. What the hell am I supposed to tell my wife and kids? No money for food this week!!! And forget about making the rent!!!"

I am really on a roll at this point. Consequences are the farthest thing from my mind. And there I stand just raving and ranting about my predicament. Now, I happen to be wearing one of those big Carpenter's belts. You know, the kind that has a hammer, screwdriver, and tape measure on it. And that hammer is just itchin' to come out of that belt!

With a rageful, furious head of steam, I suddenly decide to pay that contractor boss of mine a visit. No way this situation is going to go down easily with me! A show of force is exactly what the doctor ordered, damn it to hell! And I am just the one to do it!

I open the door to my boss's office, and see him sitting quietly behind his big, beautiful, shiny oak desk... chatting in a pleasant, happy voice to one of his suppliers. "Sure you can be a little late on that delivery," he gushes, "I know you'll get it to me as soon as you can." He is barely finished getting the words out when I explode toward him with my hammer raised.

Out of the corner of his eye, he sees me and flinches, tossing his cell phone in the air, as my hammer comes smashing down on his big shiny oak desk! "Crash!!" goes my trusty hammer as it buckles his desk, leaving a huge, nasty crack right down the middle!!

"*NOW* do I have your god damned attention??!!" I scream, wide eyed and furious. "Ten years I've put in at this job," I wail. "Ten years working out in the ice, and snow and rain, day after day – even when I was sick as a dog – so YOU could make your deadlines. And this is what I get???!!!" My rageful tirade has me pacing to and fro as the boss cringes behind his broken desk. Suddenly I find myself in front of a portrait of his wife and kids hanging on the wall. I slap it ferociously with my right hand, sending it careening off its hook and on to the floor in front of me. My rage has no bounds at this point.

But now as I turn around, I see that the boss is on his phone again. Who's he calling this time? He's calling the cops and when they come my day is about to get much, much worse.

As I stare at him in combined terror and disbelief, I know what's happening next! Consequences, Consequences, Consequences!!! When the police get here, I will immediately be placed in handcuffs, and thrown into the back of a police car. I am likely going to spend the night in jail. My boss will likely get an order of protection against me. I'll be lucky if I get my tool box back off his property. I am immediately out of a job. No reference for my next job. I'll have to pay for the oak desk I damaged. And for the portrait I knocked off the wall. And who knows how much time I'll spend in Court with lawyer's fees and lost time. All because I chose to take the path of Physical Aggression. The Consequences just keep on coming and coming. Hmmm. Maybe that other approach – the assertive one – might have been worth trying after all.

By the way, there is another possible approach to dealing with this situation. I call it the Passive Aggressive approach. And here's how that one goes. (It's no more effective than the Physically and Verbally Aggressive approach, but at least the cops don't get involved!)

So the boss has just finished telling me how he's going to have to cut me $5 an hour. And how the company hasn't been selling houses. Yada yada yada. My response this time goes something like this: "Sure. I get it boss. I know the economy hasn't been good. You gotta do what you gotta do." My boss looks at me, relieved and thankful that I understand… that I'm basically OK with it, and that he won't have to deal with any unpleasant exchange between the two of us. He waves to me as he leaves. "Thanks Dave. Have a great day."

But inside, my guts are churning. I'm not about to race down to his office with my hammer and do a number on his oak desk. But inside I am definitely pissed off. "How can they do this to me," I wail to no one in particular. "Ten years of busting my ass for these people, and this is what I get?? A pay cut that's gonna take food out of my family's mouths??!!"

By the time I get to the house I'm working on today, my anger has really been stoked. Though I didn't have the nerve to express my frustration in words to my boss… I am clearly not on board with this new development. "How dare they do this to me??" I lament as

I look at the stacks of sheetrock I'm supposed to be tacking up on the walls of the new house I've just framed.

"I know how I can save that SOB some money," I chuckle in a devilish way. "I'll save him money on sheetrock screws. Instead of putting 12 sheetrock screws in that slab I'm putting up, I'll nail 4 screws in. That'll save him money on 8 sheetrock screws. And when that damn slab of sheetrock falls off, he can get some other asshole to put it back up. Because I'll be long gone!" In other words, in my Passive Aggressive rage, I'm basically giving the boss the finger... doing a crappy job – just to get back at him for the pay cut that I didn't have the courage to address with him in the first place.

Another way I could "give him the finger" would be this way: "So the boss wants me to put two coats of paint on the basement walls. I'll save him some money on paint. I'll just do one coat. Besides, the ballgame is on the radio, and I think I'll just take a break and tune it in while I'm enjoying an extra long lunch!"

Are there consequences to this behavior? Ultimately, I'd have to think that the boss will see that the quality of my work is slipping. And that can't be a good thing. Besides which I will become more and more unhappy, going in every day to a job where I feel ill-used and frustrated now that I'm being paid less.

Bottom line: The Assertive approach is the one way that can at least give us a shot at a happy ending. Everything else pretty much dooms us to consequences we will NOT be happy to endure.

How about another example of how to deal with a difficult situation? Here's a situation that occurred to a young man who lived in a group home with five other young men while coming to a group therapy center to address emotional problems during the day. Let's call this young man "Joey" just for discussion sake. Each of the young men at the group home had a specific chore to do – from cleaning the bathrooms to mopping the floors. Joey's chore was to wash the dishes every Monday night. And that chore normally would take him about an hour and a half to complete.

On this particular occasion, a staff member came up to Joey on a Tuesday morning and said the following: "Joey, I know you did the dishes last night. But today is Tuesday and I need a special favor of you. Roy normally does the dishes on Tuesday nights. But today's his birthday and his family is coming up from Philadelphia to take him out for dinner to celebrate. I wonder if you wouldn't mind just doing the dishes again tonight. Just so Roy could go out with his family for his birthday. Would that be OK?"

Now here's the Assertive version of how Joey might act under the circumstances: "Gee whiz. I mean I am happy for Roy that his folks are coming up to take him out for his birthday. But I just did the dishes last night and it took me over an hour and a half to get the job done. I don't mind helping Roy out but it is a big job! I tell you what: How about I do the dishes for Roy tonight so he can go out with his family. That'll mean I did the dishes two nights in a row. So how about next week… Roy does my Monday night dishes AND his Tuesday night dishes? That way, I get a little bit of a vacation next week."

The staff member thinks for a moment and then agrees: "You got it Joey. You do Roy's Tuesday night dishes tonight… and he can do your Monday night dishes AND his Tuesday night dishes next week. That sounds fair to me."

Now that is the essence of assertiveness. Joey clearly stood up for himself in a firm but respectful manner. And his approach led to a fair resolution that all sides could live with.

But you can imagine what the Physical and Verbal Aggressive version of this story might entail! After the staff member has asked Joey to do the dishes for Roy – Joey becomes enraged. How dare the staff member ask him to do Roy's chore one night after Joey spent an hour and a half doing his own Monday night dishes!!

Joey picks up a large ceramic dinner plate from the cupboard. "You want me to do Roy's dishes tonight while he goes out for dinner??!! The night after I did all the Monday dishes??!! You can take this plate and shove it where the sun don't shine!!!" And then, in one motion, Joey hurls the large dinner plate in the direction of the staff member, barely missing the staff member's head! Joey races past the staff member, and runs out into the street in front of the group home, cursing and lashing out verbally at the staff member.

Now, as soon as the staff member regains his composure after ducking the hurtling dinner plate... he calls the you-know-who. "Is this the police?" he pleads into the phone. "Please come immediately. There's a group home resident here who almost killed me by throwing a dinner dish at my head. He's out front yelling and screaming right now. Please pick him up and bring him to the local shelter. Because I surely can't allow him to come back into the house given the circumstances." Consequences, consequences, consequences. That's what the Physical and Verbal Aggression approach gets for us. Just like with the carpenter, this young man will reap plenty of negative results for the approach he decided to take.

And then there's the Passive Aggressive approach. Check this out. Young Joey stands in front of the staff member with his head down speaking in a very low voice. "Gosh, Roy's going out to dinner with his family tonight. That's nice. So somebody's gotta do his dishes. Guess it may as well be me. Sure, I guess I'll do the Tuesday dishes tonight." The staff member expresses his deepest gratitude, but he has no idea of what Joey's really going to do tonight.

It all starts with a gnawing, painful feeling of resentment deep inside Joey's heart. And a failure to be Assertive from the start. Let's watch him as he begins the task of washing all the dishes and pots and pans on this Tuesday night. (Joey has just washed the first two dishes, and is beginning to grouse and complain over his fate.)

"Here I am washing the dishes. And Roy's out with his family celebrating his Birthday. Probably at Outback or some other place for a nice steak dinner. Maybe ice cream and cake. And here I am washing the dishes that *he* was supposed to do!"

Joey is proceeding to get angrier and more frustrated. He takes a swipe with his sponge at the next plate in his hands, half heartedly wiping away less than half the pasta sauce that coats the plate. Talking to no one in particular, he holds the plate up as though examining it. "How's this look, Roy? Look clean enough to you?" Joey says, as he angrily jams the half clean plate into the dish rack. Joey does this over and over again in the following minutes. And when he gets to the silverware, he just holds all of the forks, spoons and knives together in a bunch under the water faucet… and then jams them into the silverware rack. Within moments he's all done. Joey claps his hands and exclaims "Just eight minutes! That's all it took me to wash the dishes!" He then walks away, heading up to bed, having done a half-assed job on the dishes. It was his way of saying, "Nobody's going to make me do the dishes while Roy goes out for dinner!"

The next day, Joey's Passive Aggressive behavior catches up with him. The staff member, thinking that all the dishes are clean, yells out "Nice job on the dishes…" But suddenly stops in mid sentence. "Joey!!!" he screams as he suddenly realizes that Joey did a totally crappy job on the dishes, just leaving the appearance of having done them as he was asked to.

But the staff member's screams are unheard by Joey. He's already on the morning minibus to the clinical center. And the staff member ends up having to wash all the dishes from scratch by himself! You can bet that Joey's next interaction with the staff member will not be a happy one.

The only version of this story that produces no real consequences, is the one in which Joey stood up for himself in a firm but respectful manner. And that's what Assertiveness can get for you. A resolution that can really work for you, while avoiding the negative consequences anger usually generates.

CHAPTER 8

TAKE-AWAYS FROM ANGRY LIKE ME

Throughout the course of this book, we have touched upon everything from the triggers that ignite our Anger, and the feelings that underlie it…to the best ways to monitor it, control it and even safely discharge it. All in the name of avoiding the consequences that result when we allow the volcano inside to erupt in torrents of physical and verbal aggression.

I have shared that the seat of my *own* anger, deep inside, is the feeling of impatience that was hard wired into me as a young child, one of 11 children, who constantly found myself jockeying for position at the dinner table, waiting in line to go to the bathroom, watching the meatloaf travel ever so slowly around the table, wondering if there'd even be a morsel left for me at the end of its journey. A slow-moving shopper, a crowded doctor's office, a slow and inconsiderate counter person at the Motor Vehicles Department can all have the effect of triggering those feelings of frustration and helplessness I once shared with 10 other siblings. And the chances of me reacting in a physically and verbally aggressive manner was pretty much guaranteed.

That's why – reflecting back on my own underlying seeds to anger — I always recommend that, in addition to following all the strategies and techniques I have outlined here, it pays to try – more than anything else – to know ourselves. Even if it means seeing a therapist or counselor who might shed some light on what is hard for us to see. We need to dig deep. Just who is that person underneath the red flustered face, the expletive-spouting voice, the hurt, disrespected, emotionally distraught human being, just dying to pop that inconsiderate person in front of you right in the nose??!!

Throughout my years facilitating Anger Management sessions, I have met many people who – had they just had a small inkling of where their rage and anger resided – would have been more than able to avoid the consequences of their aggressive acts. Like the 22 year old man who got out of his car and bashed in the hood, windshield, tires and trunk of a vehicle that had cut him off only moments earlier. After the Court mandated him to see me for anger management, I got to know him over the five weeks we worked together. At one point, I actually told him that he seemed like a pretty nice guy overall. Where the hell did this rage come from? After several moments reflection, the young man began to cry, sobbing openly, saying that he had never known himself to be any different. In fact, he said tearfully, that he was always hitting someone at school, breaking someone's property, feeling outraged that he didn't have what someone else had. And if any of his classmates ever gave him lip, he gave them a "fat lip" that they'd never forget. Basically, any hint of disrespect allowed him to discharge some of that simmering, festering ball of rage that sat anchored to his inner being, hard wired into his childhood brain.

As fate would have it, this young man had suffered terribly as a young child in a family where he watched his alcoholic father beat his mother, trash the house, and often turn on him with terrifying anger. As we processed this information together, the man slowly began to see how the source of his anger was buried deep inside:

Unable to stand up to his burly, menacing father, he cowered in the corner of his home, trembling with rage himself. Watching his father throw his mother across the room, and then smash the flower arrangement she had just put together, he dared not challenge this beastly, rageful man who called himself his father. And whenever that man shoved his fist in his face, told him he'd never amount to anything, or failed to validate him for any of the good things he did – like winning a football game or getting a decent grade in a tough class – he held all of his disappointment and anger inside. Yes, and as he raged against his father deep inside, he wanted so much to "teach him a lesson" and give him some of his own medicine. But alas, he was helpless to do so. He would have been squashed like a tiny bug.

Over the years, the anger that was unable to find release against the menacing father, built up inside. Bubbling over from the pit of his stomach, it was ultimately redirected. Toward classmates. Toward neighbors. Toward his own wife and children. And finally toward the person who dared to cut him off on the road at the end of a long work day.

Comprehending this fact about himself set off a whole series of thoughts that he found helpful. "Every time you suffer the consequences of aggression, your father wins," I explained. "Because you were unable to deal with that anger years ago, you bottled it up inside. The result has been an ongoing progression of hostile acts... all energized and initiated by the anger against your father that has continued to fester deep inside." Just by talking about it during our sessions, he began to understand that this was not some shadowy emotion he could not control. Rather it was based in a sad reality, and instead of processing the pain he suffered at his father's hands, he seemed doomed to direct it elsewhere. Over and over and over again. By utilizing the strategies I have outlined here, and by processing his anger, this man is now taking control of his anger. And hopefully that will set in motion a life of genuine understanding, rather than a continuation of the blind suffering that has led to so many painful consequences for him and the ones he loves.

Sadly enough, many of us have failed to process the roots of our anger. If you don't understand where your impatience, intolerance, distrust, rage, fury and other feelings of anger come from, you are likely to commit the same acts over and over. It's a fact of life. The term blind rage is rooted in this lack of insight that allows us to helplessly and hopelessly continue on our pathetic path of pain and self destruction.

Childhood is such a difficult journey to navigate. As I often tell my anger management participants, we all have a "file drawer" filled with our memories, feelings, hopes, dreams and beliefs about ourselves. As a long time Psychotherapist I am pretty strong in my current level of self belief and self esteem. If someone tells me today that I'm "a piece of crap who will never amount to anything," I simply pull out that file drawer. I glance at its thousands of files momentarily and then close it up. "Nope," I say. "You've got it all wrong. I know that isn't true about me."

But when you're a defenseless 7 year old child, your "file drawer" has maybe three or four files in it. One involves what you want for Christmas; another involves who's coming to your Birthday party: and then, oh yes, there's that file from your father or mother that says you're a "lazy, good for nothing bum who should never have been born." Even if you've never done anything to deserve that kind of treatment! I myself had a drawer like that. Yes, I had a father who was verbally and physically abusive to me and delighted in giving me weekend errands and chores so that when my friends came by to ask me to play baseball, he could respond: "No, David has to rake the lawn, and if he has any time left, he'll be painting the garage. Sorry. He can't play today." In addition to being humiliating, his brutality toward me fostered a confused hatred in me. I couldn't strike back at him. He was a giant, and I was just a kid.

And God knows, I tried to love him. It's in the nature of a child to try to love those upon whom he or she relies for food, shelter and validation. But instead over the years, I fostered an intense dislike for him. Only my Mother's support, love, and validation enabled me to navigate that difficult time. I was able ultimately to externalize these feelings, understanding that the problem was more with my father, than it was with me. As it is, I still have anger issues that I must continually work on. I understand that my chronic impatience and testiness have their roots in my simmering anger against my father, along with my frustration at being one of 11 children in a house with little food and one bathroom – neither of which I myself could control. I use the strategies I've outlined in this book every day of my life to avoid the consequences of going over the top and expressing my anger in verbal or physical aggression.

Some of us are lucky not to have to deal with ongoing thoughts and memories like the ones I've described. But for many of us, that hurtful, painful assessment by parents and caretakers – whether said in anger or not – sows the seeds of anger, fear and frustration that can come back to provide a blueprint for our behaviors in years to come. In some cases, the seeds blossom into anxiety or depression. And in many of us, the seeds develop as thorny cactus plants that tear at us inside, and demand release. Even if it's at the expense of innocent people.

As I look back over the years, I have seen so many people sadly destroyed by the anger that was spawned from their own unique frustration and pain. And they don't have a clue about where it comes from. Even worse, they often don't care to do what you are doing right now – trying to learn strategies to avoid the consequences of unbridled anger.

Most recently, I have watched another young patient turn festering rage against his self centered and verbally abusive father – a man who abandoned him at a young age — into an affinity toward violence and a desire to lash out at the vulnerable and those who don't share his values and point of view. If he would even begin to use my Anger Pyramid to monitor his behaviors, he might notice something interesting: the triggers that caused his blood to boil are not rooted in any specific personal affronts or attacks by other individuals. Rather he has simply found an easy, faceless target at which to direct the wrath he would have loved to communicate to his father. Again, a child who is subjected to parental abuse, whether verbal or physical, is too vulnerable himself to strike back at a mother or father whom he both fears and loves. The result is being mindlessly sentenced to a life of unresolved hatred, fury, anger and rage that will likely find its target sooner or later in some person who crosses that abused child's path.

Of course sometimes the anger we develop at the hands of brutal fathers and mothers is turned inward. And that can be even more tragic than lashing out at others. It can lead to self recrimination, hopelessness, depression – even thoughts of suicide. All because we can't cope with the pain that has been inflicted upon us by people who themselves were so badly damaged, they turned their own anger and frustration onto us.

A colleague of mine struggled to help a male patient understand that the anger and frustration he felt against a belligerent, angry father was innocently sown into the fabric of his life. He began to turn against himself, wondering if life was even worth living. Maybe his father was right. Maybe he *is* a weak, useless loser who deserves to be emotionally beaten up, abandoned by girlfriends, and doomed to fail in his life. Only by comprehending that the real culprit here was his drug addicted, sadistic and pathetic father – victimized by his own painful past – could this young man begin to release his self defeating feelings. He has since used this processing to help himself move forward in his life as well.

When looking inside to conquer our anger issues, let's not fail to take a closer look at the world around us as well. The seeds of our anger – and the hard wired triggers from childhood experiences

– do often reside deep inside us and contribute toward our view of the world. But let's not forget that the world itself offers circumstances and situations that often help ignite those feelings of anger and rage inside. Especially in today's age of cell phone communication, internet access and instant media coverage. I can't ever forget the female patient who broke up with her long time boyfriend over a simple text message. A mere text message!! She texted a message about getting together that evening. He texted back a response about the time being late. She took that as a rebuff, and that he didn't really want to see her anymore. He texted back that if she felt that way, she could just take a flying leap. Upset, she told him to go to hell. And presto! A promising relationship went up in flames. Wow!

If communication that includes seeing the person's facial expressions and body language while they are speaking to us is often inadequate… how much more difficult and inadequate must it be to derive any kind of sense from a mere text message? Yet day after day, millions of us rely on text messages to relay our thoughts, feelings and plans to other people. If that isn't the blindest form of communication ever, I don't know what is. No wonder so much verbal aggression finds expression in our lives. If we are not aware of our own personal triggers, while monitoring them constantly through the techniques I have outlined in this book, we have little chance of avoiding the consequences of verbal aggression when we can't even understand what others are trying to communicate. It's that easy to be triggered. And broken relationships are just the start. How about the fact that many, many people – especially adolescents –use text messaging to bully and denigrate others? Giving them an easy way to unleash anger they have deep inside.

One very young female patient of mine hid under the covers every morning rather than go to school because of vile and abusive text messages she received from a bullying classmate. It wasn't until I demanded that the Principal monitor in-school bullying toward this young girl that the perpetrator was exposed. Interestingly enough, the perpetrator was a depressed young girl whose mother was brutally aggressive toward *her*. That situation truly illustrates my belief in the devastating role that parental abuse plays in the making of an angry, aggressive person. Unable to unleash her anger against her overbearing, alcoholic mother, this young girl chose to direct her rage against an innocent classmate who had been unable to strike back. That young girl was soon provided individual and family counseling that would hopefully help her to understand, and control, her angry impulses in the future.

In today's political climate you can also feel that there is almost a kind of "permission" to express the anger we may have deep inside… to discharge it in the form of physical or verbal aggression. It's seen in verbal aggression against people who are different from us, people who have different political beliefs, or even different cultural backgrounds. Just look at the cable news stations to see how low we are willing to go as a nation, almost savoring verbal attacks on one another both on the air and in the community. And look at the expressions of physical aggression with physical violence, mass shootings, destruction of property and other once unthinkable acts of aggression. One has to wonder where it will all end.

Well my task is not to end the world's physical and verbal aggression, although I would love to see that happen in my lifetime, as unlikely as that may be. No, my hope is that people like you and I will wake up to the anger inside us, and realize that we can change the trajectory of our lives. That by following the strategies and skills I have outlined here, we do have a shot at avoiding the kind of verbal and physical aggression that can take away all the good, and leave us suffering the consequences of actions that, I believe, we truly can control.

It all starts with our determination to change. Are *you* willing to try? I know I am trying. Let's join together to make our lives more about gratitude, hope and love. And less about getting angry, aggressive and even. Who knows? Maybe others will follow our path to a happier, less aggressive life where the consequences of our actions don't include broken relationships, jail time, lost jobs and similar negative results. Wishing you all the best on your journey!

OVERVIEW

Let's face it. Some self help books can be preachy, nuts and bolts, yawn-inducing diatribes on what to do and what not to do. Angry Like Me is written in an irreverent, sometimes funny, often eye opening style that takes the reader beyond nuts and bolts advice to an intimate understanding of this painful but controllable mental health issue. But there's also a unique twist here: As a Licensed Psychotherapist, I share MY OWN Anger issues… from raging at the couple in the apartment above me with their ultra loud Saturday night parties… and cursing my Doctor under my breath in his crowded waiting room after an hour of reading Ladies Home Journal…. to wanting to toss loose change in the face of an elderly shopper holding me up in line as he searches for a 5 cent coupon. I share my own strategies and coping skills to help the reader avoid the Consequences of unbridled Anger just as I have.

ABOUT THE AUTHOR

A 1973 graduate of The University of California, Berkeley, David Haviland spent the first 25 years of his professional career as an Advertising Creative Director, writing radio, TV and newspaper ads for major corporate clients. In the early 1980's David awakened to the vital importance of public service when he had the opportunity to promote social programs like The Harlem Children's Zone and St. Patrick's Cathedral's Our Neighbors outreach to Manhattan's elderly. Recognizing his true calling in the faces of the people he helped, and inspired by his mother Muriel's work with New York's AIDS patients, David returned to college to obtain his Masters in Social Work at SUNY Albany. From that point, he never looked back, working with patients on the psychiatric unit at St. Francis Hospital in Poughkeepsie, and ultimately starting his 5 session Anger Management Program which continues to receive referrals from Courts, attorneys, and social service organizations throughout the Hudson Valley. Committed to making a difference in the lives of others, David lives happily in Cold Spring, NY with his artist wife Debbie and his two daughters, Stephanie and Rebecca.

Made in the USA
Middletown, DE
28 April 2019